D1326108

The
CLASSIC
GUIDE
TO ROWING

The
CLASSIC
GUIDE
TO ROWING

RUDOLF CHAMBERS LEHMANN

AMBERLEY

As a slight token of friendship I dedicate this book to Mr Herbert Thomas Steward, Chairman of the Amateur Rowing Association, Chairman of the Committee of Management, Henley Regatta and President of the Leander Club.

This edition published 2016

Amberley Publishing
The Hill, Stroud, Gloucestershire, GL5 4EP
www.amberley-books.com

Copyright © Amberley Publishing, 2016

All rights reserved. No part of this book may be reprinted or reproduced or utilised in any form or by any electronic, mechanical or other means, now known or hereafter invented, including photocopying and recording, or in any information storage or retrieval system, without the permission in writing from the Publishers.

ISBN 978 1 4456 4906 1 (print)
ISBN 978 1 4456 4907 8 (ebook)

British Library Cataloguing in Publication Data.
A catalogue record for this book is available from the British Library.

Typesetting by Amberley Publishing.
Printed in Great Britain.

Contents

Editor's Note

Rowing was originally used as a mode of transport for trade and naval warfare. Rowing also initially became popular for recreational activity rather than for racing. Modern competitive rowing as we know it today can be traced back to the eighteenth century when races were held on the River Thames. With the creation of boat clubs in the likes of the University of Oxford and University of Cambridge, Eton College and Westminster School amateur competitive racing became established.

Rowing is one of the oldest Olympic sports and has been competed for since 1900. Although a male-dominated sport, women's rowing can be traced back to the nineteenth century but it was not until the 1976 Olympics that female rowing competitors could take part. There are now in the twenty-first century events for those with physical disabilities known as adaptive rowing. These however are not mentioned within the book as the rowing of the era R. C. Lehmann focusses on the predominantly male discipline. The method, training and the various different types of rowing like sculling are discussed. With input from Guy Nickalls, G. L. Davis, C. M. Pitman, W. E. Crum and E. G. Blackmore, Lehmann, best placed to coach, seeks to provide as much guidance as a book can give to the rowing novice. *The Classic Guide To Rowing* gives a glimpse into the world of rowing in the twentieth century, showing how techniques, still used today, first originated.

Vanessa Le, MA
Editor

Author's Preface

My thanks are due to the proprietors of the *Daily News* and of the *English Illustrated Magazine* for permission to include in this book the substance of articles originally contributed to their columns.

For the rest, I have endeavoured to make the rowing instructions which will be found in this book as concise as was compatible with perfect clearness, assuming at all times that I was addressing myself first of all to the novice. No doubt other oarsmen will differ here and there from my conclusions. Absolute unanimity on every detail of rowing is not to be expected.

All I can do is to assure my readers that nothing has been set down here the truth and accuracy of which I have not proved – at least, to my own satisfaction.

The illustrations are reproduced from photographs by Messrs Stearn, of Cambridge; Messrs Gillman, of Oxford; Messrs Marsh, of Henley-on-Thames; Messrs Hills and Saunders, of Eton; Messrs Pach Brothers, of Cambridge (Mass.); and Mr J. G. Williams, of East Molesey.

R. C. L.
October, 1897

Introduction

My object in the following pages will be not merely to give such hints to the novice as may enable him, so far as book-learning can affect the purpose, to master the rudiments of oarsmanship, but also to commend to him the sport of rowing from the point of view of those enthusiasts who regard it as a noble open-air exercise, fruitful in lessons of strength, courage, discipline, and endurance, and as an art which requires on the part of its votaries a sense of rhythm, a perfect balance and symmetry of bodily effort, and the graceful control and repose which lend an appearance of ease to the application of the highest muscular energy. Much has to be suffered and many difficulties have to be overcome before the raw tiro, whose fantastic contortions in a tub pair excite the derision of the spectators, can approach to the power, effectiveness and grace of a Crum or a Gold; but, given a healthy frame and sound organs inured to fatigue by the sports of English boyhood, given also an alert intelligence, there is no reason in the nature of things why oarsmanship should not eventually become both an exercise and a pleasure. And when I speak of oarsmanship, I mean the combined form of it in pairs, in fours, and in eight-oared racing boats.

Of sculling I do not presume to speak, but those who are curious on this point may be referred to the remarks of Mr Guy Nickalls in a later chapter. But of rowing I can speak, if not with authority, at any rate with experience, for during twenty-three years of my life I have not only rowed in a constant succession of boat races, amounting now to about 200, but I have watched rowing wherever it was to be seen, and have, year after year, been privileged to utter words of instruction to innumerable crews on the Cam, the Isis, and the Thames. If, then, the novice will commit himself for a time to my guidance, I will endeavour to initiate him into the art and mystery of rowing. If he decides afterwards to join the fraternity of its votaries, I can promise him that his reward will not be small. He may not win fame, and he will certainly not increase his store of wealth, but when his time of action is past and he joins the great army of 'have-beens,' he will find, as he looks back upon his career, that his hours of leisure have been spent in an exercise which has enlarged his frame and strengthened his limbs, that he has drunk delight of battle with his peers in many a hard-fought race, that he has learnt what it means to be in perfect health and condition, with every sinew strung, and all his manly energies braced for contests of strength and endurance, and that he has bound to himself by the strongest possible ties a body of staunch and loyal friends whose worth has been proved under all sorts of conditions, through many days of united effort.

It has often been objected to rowing, either by those who have never rowed, or by those who having rowed have allowed themselves to sink prematurely into sloth and decay, that the sport in the case of most men can last only for a very few years, and that having warred, not without glory, up to the age of about twenty-five, they must then hang their oars upon the wall and pass the remainder of their lives in an envious contemplation of the exploits of old but unwearied cricketers. Judging merely by my own personal experience, I am entitled to pronounce these lamentations baseless and misleading, for I have been able to row with pleasure even in racing boats during the whole period of nineteen years that has elapsed since I took

The Oxford and Cambridge Boat Race, 1894.

my degree at Cambridge. But I can refer to higher examples, for I have seen the Grand Challenge Cup and the Stewards' Cup at Henley Regatta either rowed for with credit, or won by men whose age cannot have been far, if at all, short of forty years, and of men who won big races when they were thirty years old the examples are innumerable. But putting actual racing aside, there is in skilled rowing a peculiar pleasure (even though the craft rowed in may merely be a fixed seat gig) which, as it seems to me, puts it on a higher plane than most other exercises. The watermanship which enables a party of veterans to steer their boat deftly in and out of a lock, to swing her easily along the reaches, while unskilled youths are toiling and panting astern, is, after all, no mean accomplishment. And in recent years rowing has taken a leaf out of the book of cricket. Scattered up and down the banks of the Thames are many pleasant houses in which, during the summer, men who can row are favoured guests, either with a view to their forming crews to take part in local regattas, or merely for the purpose of pleasure-rowing in scenes remote from the dust and turmoil of the city. Let no one, therefore, be repelled from oarsmanship because he thinks that the sport will last him through only a few years of his life. If he marries and settles down and becomes a busy man, he will enjoy his holiday on the Thames fully as much as his cricketing brothers enjoy theirs on some country cricket field.

Of the early history of boats and boat-racing it is not necessary to say very much. It is enough to know that the written Cambridge records date back to 1827, though it is certain that racing must have begun some years previously; that Oxford can point to 1822 as one of the earliest years of their college races; that the two universities raced against one another for the first time in 1829; and that Henley Regatta was established in 1839, when the Grand Challenge Cup was won by First Trinity, Cambridge.

Those who desire to go still further back, have the authority of Virgil for stating that the Trojans under Aeneas could organize and carry through what Professor Conington, in his version of the 'Aeneid,' calls 'a rivalry of naval speed.' The account of this famous regatta is given with a spirit and a richness of detail that put to shame even the most modern historians of aquatic prowess. After reading how Gyas, the captain and coach of the Chimæra –

> Huge bulk, a city scarce so large,
> With Dardan rowers in triple bank,
> The tiers ascending rank o'er rank

– how Gyas, as I say, justly indignant at the ineptitude and cowardice of his coxswain, hurled him from the vessel, and himself assumed the helm at a critical point of the race, it is a mere paltering with the emotions to be told, for instance, that 'Mr Pechell, who owes much to the teaching of Goosey Driver, steered a very good course,' or that he 'began to make the shoot for Barnes Bridge a trifle too soon.' How, too, can the statement that 'both crews started simultaneously, Cambridge, if anything, striking the water first' compare with the passage which tells us (I quote again from Professor Conington) how

> At the trumpet's piercing sound,
> All from their barriers onward bound,
> Upsoars to heaven the oarsman's shout,
> The upturned billows froth and spout;
> In level lines they plough the deep—
> All ocean yawns as on they sweep.

It may be noted in passing that no one else seems to have felt in the least inclined to yawn, for

> With plaudits loud and clamorous zeal
> Echoes the woodland round;
> The pent shores roll the thunder peal –
> The stricken rocks rebound;

which seems, if the criticism may be permitted, a curious proceeding even for a stricken rock during the progress of a boat race. Finally, a touch of religious romance is added when we learn that the final result was due, not to the unaided efforts of the straining crew, but to the intervention of Portunus, the Harbour God, who, moved by the prayer of Cloanthus, captain of the Scylla, pushed that barque along and carried her triumphantly first into the haven – invidious conduct which does not appear to have caused the least complaint among the defeated crews, or to have prevented Cloanthus from being proclaimed the victor of the day. Only on one occasion (in 1859) has Father Thames similarly exerted himself to the advantage of one of the university crews, for during the boat race of that year he swamped the Cambridge ship beneath his mighty waves, and sped Oxford safely to Mortlake. Lord Justice A. L. Smith, among others, still lives, though he was unable to swim, to tell the exciting tale.

Before I take leave of this Virgilian race, I may perhaps, even at this late date, be permitted as a brother coach to commiserate the impulsive but unfortunate Gyas on the difficulties he must have encountered in coaching the crew of a trireme. Not less do I pity his oarsmen, of whom the two lower ranks must have suffered seriously as to their backs from the feet of those placed above them, while the length and weight of the oars used by the top rank must have made good form and accurate time almost impossible. A Cambridge poet, Mr R. H. Forster, has sung the woes of the Athenian triremists and their instructor –

> Just imagine a crew of a hundred or two
> Shoved three deep in a kind of a barge,
> Like a cargo of kegs, with no room for their legs,
> And oars inconveniently large.
> Quoth he, 'παντες προσω' and they try to do so.
> At the sight the poor coach's brains addle;
> So muttering 'οιμοι,' he shouts out 'ἑτοιμοι,'
> And whatever the Greek is for 'paddle.'
> Now do look alive, number ninety and five,
> You're 'sugaring,' work seems to bore you;
> You are late, you are late, number twenty and eight,
> Keep your eyes on the man that's before you.

So much for the trireme. But neither the Greeks nor any other race thought of adapting their boats merely to purposes of racing until the English, with their inveterate passion for open-air exercise, took the matter in hand. African war canoes have been known to race, but their primary object is still the destruction of rival canoes together with their dusky freight. In Venice the gondoliers are matched annually against one another, but both the gondola and the sandolo remain what they always have been – mere vessels for the conveyance of passengers and goods. The man who would make war in a racing ship would justly be relegated to Hanwell, and to carry passengers, or even one 'passenger,' in such a boat is generally looked upon as a certain presage of defeat. Consider for a moment. The modern racing ship (eight, four, pair, or single) is a frail, elongated, graceful piece of cabinet work, held together by thin stays, small bolts, and copper nails, and separating you from the water in which it floats by an eighth of an inch of Mexican cedar. The whole weight of the sculling boat, built by Jack Clasper, in which Harding won the Searle Memorial Cup, was only nineteen pounds, i.e. about 112 pounds lighter than the man it carried. Considering the amount of labour and trained skill that go towards the construction of these beautiful machines, the price cannot be said to be heavy. Most builders will turn you out a sculling-boat for from £12 to £15, a pair for about £20, a four for £33, and an eight for £55. But the development of the racing type to its present perfection has taken many years. Little did the undergraduates who, in 1829, drove their ponderous man-of-war's galleys from Hambledon Lock to Henley Bridge, while the stricken hills of the Thames Valley rebounded to the shouts of the spectators – little did they imagine that their successors, rowing on movable seats and with rowlocks projecting far beyond the side would speed in delicate barques, of arrowy shape and almost arrowy swiftness, from Putney to Mortlake – in barques so light and crank that, built as they are without a keel, they would overturn in a moment if the balance of the oars were removed. The improvements were very gradual. In 1846 the University Race was rowed for the first time in boats with outriggers. That innovation had, however, been creeping in for some years before that. Mr Hugh Hammersley, who rowed in the Oriel boat which started head of the river at Oxford in 1843, has told me that in that year the University College boat, stroked by the famous Fletcher Menzies, was fitted with outriggers at stroke and bow; and the bump by which University displaced Oriel was generally ascribed to the new invention.

In 1857 the University race was rowed in boats without a keel, and oars with a round loom were used for the first time by both crews. At the Henley Regatta of the preceding year the Royal Chester Rowing Club had entered a crew rowing in this novel style of keelless boat for the Grand Challenge and the Ladies' Cups. Her length was only fifty-four feet, and her builder was Mat Taylor, a name celebrated in the annals of boatbuilding, for it is to him, in the first instance, that our present type of racing boat owes its existence. 'The Chester men,' Mr W. B. Woodgate tells us in his Badminton book on boating, 'could not sit their boat in the least; they flopped their blades along the water on the recovery in a manner which few junior crews at minor regattas would now be guilty of; but they rowed well away from their opponents, who were only College crews.' They won, as a matter of fact, both the events for which they entered.

One might have thought that with this invention improvements would have ceased. But in course of time the practical experience of rowing men suggested to them that if they slid on their seats, both the length and power of their stroke through the water would be increased. At first they greased their fixed seats, and slid on those. But it was found that the strain caused by this method exhausted a crew. In 1871 a crew of professionals used a seat that slid on the thwarts, and beat a crew that was generally held to be superior, and from that moment slides, as we now know them, came into general use. In 1873 the university crews rowed on sliding seats for the first time. Since then the length of the slide has been increased from about nine inches to fifteen inches, or even more, a change which has made the task of the boatbuilder in providing floating capacity more difficult; but in all essentials the type of boat remains the same. It ought to be added that the Americans, to a large extent, use boats moulded out of papier mâché, but this variation has never obtained favour in England, though boats built in this manner by the well-known Waters of Troy (USA) have been seen on English rivers. The Columbia College crew won the Visitors' Cup at Henley in 1878 in a paper boat, and she was afterwards bought by First Trinity, Cambridge, but she never won a race again.

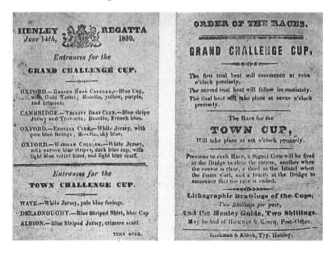

The First Henley Regatta.

First Lessons on Fixed Seats

If the tiro who aspires to be an oarsman has ever seen a really good eight-oared crew in motion on the water, he will probably have been impressed not so much by the power and the pace of it as by the remarkable ease with which the whole complicated series of movements that go to make up a stroke is performed. The eight blades grip the water at the same moment with a perfect precision, making a deep white swirl as they sweep through; the bodies swing back with a free and springy motion; the slides move steadily; and almost before one has realized that a stroke has been begun, the hands have come squarely home to the chest and have been shot out again to the full extent of the arms, the blades leaving the water without a splash. Then with a balanced swing the bodies move forward again, the oar blades all in a level line on either side, and, presto! another stroke has been started. Nothing in these movements is violent or jerky; there are no contortions – at least the tiro can see none, though the coach may be shouting instructions as to backs and shoulders and elbows – and the boat glides on her way without a pause or check.

What sort of spectacle, on the other hand, is afforded by a thoroughly bad eight? The men composing it have chests and backs together with the usual complement of limbs that make up a human being; they are provided with oars; their ship is built of cedar and fitted with slides and outriggers – in short, as they sit at ease in their boat, they resemble in all outward details the crew we have just been considering. But watch them when they begin to row. Where now are the balance, the rhythm, the level flash of blades on the feather, the crisp beginning, the dashing and almost contemptuous freedom of bodies and hands in motion, the even and unsplashing progress of the ship herself? All these have vanished, and in their place we see a boat rolling like an Atlantic liner, oars dribbling feebly along the water or soaring wildly above it, each striking for the beginning at the sweet will of the man who wields it, without regard to anybody else; eight bodies, cramped and contorted almost out of the semblance of humanity, shuffling, tumbling, and screwing, while on eight faces a look of agony bears witness to such tortures as few except Englishmen can continue to suffer without mutiny or complaint. It is not a noble or an inspiring sight; but it may be seen at Oxford or at Cambridge, on tidal waters, and even at Henley Regatta.

What, then, is the main cause of the difference between these two crews? It lies in good style – style which is present in the one crew and absent from the other. And this style in the rowing sense merely sums up the result, whether to individuals or to a crew, of long and patient teaching founded upon principles the correctness of which has been established ever since rowing became not merely an exercise, but a science in keelless racing ships. And here one comment may be added. It is the habit of every generation of rowing men to imagine that they have invented rowing all over again, and have at last, by their own intelligence and energy, established its principles on a firm foundation. Within my own experience, five at least of these generations believed that for the first time the virtues of legwork had been revealed to them, four thought they had made out a patent in the matter of body swing, and six were convinced that they had discovered length of stroke and firmness of beginning. In the eyes of these young gentlemen, the veterans whom they occasionally condescended to invite to their practice were harmless and well-meaning enthusiasts, who might have made a figure in their day, but who were, of course, utterly unable to appreciate the niceties of rowing as developed by their brilliant and skilful successors. Amiable presumption of youth and innocence! The fact is, of course, that the main principles of good rowing are the same now as they have always been, on long slides or on short slides, or even on fixed seats. And, personally, I have always found that the hints I gathered from such men as Dr Warre, Mr W. B. Woodgate, Mr J. C. Tinne, or Sir John Edwards-Moss, whose active rowing days were over before sliding seats came into use, were invaluable to me in the coaching of crews.

How is a novice to be taught so that he may someday take his seat with credit in a good crew? I answer that there is no royal road; he must pass through a long period of practice, often so dull that all his patience will be required to carry him through it. His progress will be so slow, that he will sometimes feel he is making no headway at all; but it will be sure none the less, and some day, if he has in him the makings of an oar, he will realize, to his delight, that his joints move freely, that his muscles are supple, that his limbs obey his brain immediately – that, in short, the various movements he has been striving so hard to acquire have become easy and natural to him, and that he can go through them without the painful exercise of deliberate thought at every moment of their recurrence.

Every oarsman must begin on fixed seats. This statement is to an English public school or university oar a mere platitude; but in America, and even in some of our English clubs outside the universities, its force and necessity have been lost sight of. Here and there may be found a born oar, whose limbs and body do not require an arduous discipline; but in the case of ordinary average men like the immense majority of us, it is impossible, I believe, to acquire correct body movement without a stage, more or less prolonged, of practice in fixed-seat rowing. For it is on fixed seats alone that a man can learn that free and solid swing which is essential to good oarsmanship on slides.

I will, therefore, ask my novice reader to imagine that he is seated on one of the thwarts of a fixed-seat tub-pair, while I deceive myself into the belief that I am coaching him from its stern. My first duty will be to see that all his implements are sound and true and correct, since it is probable that faults are often due as much to the use of weak or defective materials as to any other cause. I must satisfy myself that his oar is stiff and of a proper length; that when pressed against the thole in a natural position it can grip the water firmly and come through it squarely; that the stretcher is properly set, and that the straps pass tightly over the root of the toes. I must also see that he is properly dressed, and not constricted about the waist by impeding buttons. A belt is never permissible. Now for instruction –

1. Sit erect on the aft edge of your seat, exactly opposite the point at which your heels touch the stretcher. The feet must be placed firm and flat upon the stretcher, the heels touching one another, and forming an angle of about forty-five degrees. The knees must be bent to about one-third of their scope, and set a shoulder's breadth apart. Shoulders must be well set back, the chest open, and the stomach well set out.

2. Now swing your body slowly forward as far as you are able from the hips, without bending the back, being careful to let your head swing with your body. Repeat this movement several times without holding the oar.

(Note. – The ideal swing is that which takes the whole unbending body full forward till it is down between the knees. This, to a novice, is impossible, and the coach must therefore be content to see the first efforts at swing very short. It is better that this should be so than that a man should prematurely attain length by bending his back, doubling in his stomach, and over-reaching with his shoulders, faults that, once acquired, it is extremely difficult to eradicate.)

The swing must be slow and balanced, for 'the time occupied in coming forward should be the body's rest, when the easy, measured swing, erect head, braced shoulders, and open chest, enable heart and lungs to work freely and easily, in preparation for a defined beginning of the next stroke.' (From an article by Mr S. Le Blanc Smith.)

3. Take hold of your oar, the fingers passing round it, thumbs underneath, and the hands one hand's-breadth apart. The grip on the oar should be a finger-grip, not the vice-like hold that cramps all the muscles of the arm. It is important, too, to remember that, while the arms are presumably of the same length, the outside hand (i.e. the hand at the end of the oar) has, during stroke and swing forward, to pass through a larger arc than the inside hand. The inside wrist should, therefore, be slightly arched even at the beginning of the stroke, thus shortening the inside arm, but without impairing its use during the stroke. This arch, too, will give the inside hand a greater leverage and ease for performing the work of feathering, which devolves mainly upon it.

4. Draw your oar handle slowly in till the roots of the thumbs touch the chest, the elbows passing close to the sides, and the body maintaining the erect position described in instruction 1, but slightly inclined beyond the perpendicular. I assume that the blade of the oar is covered in the water in the position it would have at the finish of a stroke.

5. Drop your hands; in fact, not merely the hands, but the forearms and hands together. This movement will take the oar clean and square out of the water.

6. Turn your wrists, more particularly the inside wrist, with a quick sharp turn. This movement will feather the oar.

7. Without attempting to move your body, shoot your hands sharply out to the full extent of your arms, taking care to keep the blade of the oar well clear of the water.

Repeat these last three movements several times, at first separately, then in combination.

(Note. – These three movements are sometimes spoken of incorrectly as the finish of the stroke. Properly speaking, however, the finish, as distinguished from the beginning, is that part of the stroke which is rowed through the water from the moment the arms begin to bend until the hands come in to the chest. The movements I have described are in reality part of the recovery, i.e. they are the movements necessary to enable the oarsman's body to recover itself after the strain of one stroke, and to prepare for the next. Smartly performed, as they ought to be, they have all the appearance of one quick motion. As to the dropping of the hands, the novice must practise this so as to get his oar square and clean out of the water. It is, however, necessary to guard against exaggerating it into the pump-handle or coffee-grinding style, which merely wastes energy and time. Later on, when an oarsman is rowing in a light racing ship, a very slight pressure will enable him to release his oar, the movement and elasticity of the boat helping him.)

8. You have now taken the blade out of the water, feathered it, and have shot your hands away, the blade still on the feather, to a point beyond the knees. In so doing you will have released your body, which you must now swing forward slowly and at a perfectly even pace, in a solid column from the hips, as described in instruction 2.

9. Obviously, if you keep your arms stiff in the shoulder sockets, you will eventually, as your body swings down, force your hands against the stretcher, or into the bottom of the boat, with the blade of the oar soaring to the level of your head. To avoid this windmill performance let your hands, especially the inside hand, rest lightly on the oar handle, and as the body swings down let the hands gradually rise, i.e. let the angle that the arms make with the body increase. You will thus, by the time you have finished your swing, have brought the blade close to the water, in readiness to grip the beginning without the loss of a fraction of a second.

10. During the foregoing manoeuvre keep your arms absolutely straight from shoulder to wrist. Many oarsmen, knowing that they have to get hold of the beginning, cramp their arm muscles and bend their elbows as they swing forward, the strain giving them a fictitious feeling

of strength. But this is pure delusion, and can only result in waste, both of energy and of time.

11. As you swing, use the inside arm and hand to shove against the oar. You will thus keep the button of the oar pressed up against the rowlock, a position it ought never to even for a moment lose; you will help to steady your swing, and you will go far towards keeping both shoulders square. Most novices and many veterans overreach badly with the outside shoulder.

12. While you are carrying out the last four instructions, your feet, save for a slight pressure against the straps during the very first part of the recovery (see instruction 23), must remain firmly planted, heel and toe, against your stretcher. During your swing you should have a distinct sense of balancing with the ball of your foot against the stretcher. This resistance of the feet on the stretcher helps to prevent you from tumbling forward in a helpless, huddled mass as you reach the limit of your forward swing.

13. As to taking the oar off the feather. Good oars vary considerably on this point. Some carry the blade back feathered the whole way, and only turn it square just in time to get the beginning of the stroke. Others turn it off the feather about halfway through, just before the hands come over the stretcher. For a novice, I certainly recommend the latter method. Turn your wrists up and square your blade very soon after the hands have cleared the knees. It will thus be easier for you to keep your button pressed against the rowlock; your hands can balance the oar better, and you will not run the risk, to which the former method renders you liable, of skying or cocking your blade just when it ought to be nearest the water, so as to catch the beginning. A good and experienced waterman, however, ought certainly to be able to keep his oar on the feather against a high wind until the last available moment. The movement of returning the blade to the square position ought to be firm and clean.

14. As the body swings, your hands ought to be at the same time stretching and reaching out as if constantly striving to touch something which is constantly evading them.

15. When you are full forward, the blade of your oar should not be quite at a right angle to the water, but the top of it ought to be very slightly inclined over, i.e. towards the stern of the boat. A blade thus held will grip the water cleaner, firmer, and with far less back-splash than a blade

held absolutely at right angles. Besides, you will obviate the danger of 'slicing' into the water and rowing too deep. At the same time, I am bound to admit that I know only a few oars who adopt this plan. One of them, however, is the present President of the Oxford University Boat Club, Mr C. K. Philips, as good a waterman as ever sat in a boat. I am quite firmly convinced that the plan is a sound one, and I believe if it were more generally followed, we should see far less of that uncomfortable and unsightly habit of back splashing, which is too often seen even in good crews.

16. I have now brought you forward to the full extent of your swing and reach. Your back is (or ought to be) straight, your shoulders are firm and braced, your chest and stomach still open, though your body is down somewhere between your open knees. Your hands have been gradually rising, and your oar blade is, therefore, close to the water. Now raise your hands a little more, not so as to splash the blade helplessly to the bottom of the river, but with a quick movement as though they were passing round a cylinder. When they get to the top of the cylinder the blade will be covered in the water. At the same moment, and without the loss of a fraction of a second, swing the body and shoulders back as though they were released from a spring, the arms remaining perfectly straight, and the feet helping by a sharp and vigorous pressure (from the ball of the foot, and the toes especially) against the stretcher. The result of these rapid combined movements will be that the blade, as it immerses itself in the water, will strike it with an irresistible force (a sort of crunch, as when you grind your heel into gravel), created by the whole weight-power of the body applied through the straight lines of the arms, and aided by all the strength of which the legs are capable. This, technically speaking, is the beginning of the stroke. The outside hand should have a good grip of the oar.

17. Swing back, as I said, with arms straight. The novice must, especially if he has muscular arms, root in his head the idea that the arms are during a great part of the stroke connecting rods, and that it is futile to endeavour to use them independently of the body weight, which is the real driving power.

18. Just before the body attains the limit of its back swing, which should be at a point a little beyond the perpendicular, begin to bend your arms for the finish of the stroke, and

bring the hands square home until the roots of the thumbs touch the chest about three inches below the separation of the ribs. Here you must be careful not to raise or depress the hands. They should sweep in to the chest in an even plane, the outside hand drawing the handle firmly home without lugging or jerking. As the hands come in, the body finishes its swing, the elbows pass close to the sides, pointing downwards, and the shoulders are rowed back and kept down. The chest must be open, but not unduly inflated at the expense of the stomach, the head erect, and the whole body carrying itself easily, gracefully, and without unnecessary stiffness.

19. Do not meet your oar, i.e. keep your body back until the hands have come in. If you pull yourself forward to meet your oar, you will certainly shorten the stroke, tire yourself prematurely, and will probably fail to get the oar clean out of the water or to clear your knees on the recovery.

20. Do not try to force down your legs and flatten the knees as if you were rowing on a sliding seat. The mere movement of the body on the back swing and the kick off the stretcher will cause a certain alteration in the bend of the knees, but this tendency should not be consciously increased. Remember that fixed-seat rowing is not now an end in itself. It is a stage towards skilled rowing on sliding seats, and its chief object is to give the novice practice in certain essential elements of the stroke, and particularly in body-swing, which could not be so easily taught, if at all, if he were to begin at once on sliding seats. Swing is still, as it always has been, all important in good rowing, and if a novice attempts to slide (for that is what it comes to) on fixed seats he will begin to shuffle and lose swing entirely.

21. Do not let your body settle down or fall away from your oar at the finish. Sit erect on your bones, and do not sink back on to your tail. The bones are the pivot on which you should swing.

22. The blade of the oar, having been fully covered at the very beginning of the stroke, must remain fully covered up to the moment that the hands are dropped. If the oarsman, when he bends his arms during the stroke, begins to depress his hands, he will row light, i.e. the blade will be partially uncovered, and will naturally lose power. On the other hand, if he raises his hands unduly, he will

cover more than the blade, and will find great difficulty in extracting it from the water properly. The outside hand should control the balance of the oar, and keep it at its proper level.

23. Now to the use of the stretcher-straps. Many coaches imagine that when they have said, 'Do not pull yourself forward by your toes against the straps,' they have exhausted all that is to be said on the matter. I venture, with all deference, to differ from them. I agree that in the earlier stages of instruction it is very useful to make men occasionally row in tub-pairs without any straps, so as to force them to develop and strengthen the muscles of stomach and legs, which ought to do the main work of the recovery. But later on, when a man is rowing in an eight, and is striving, according to the instructions of his coach, to swing his body well and freely back, he can no more recover properly without a slight toe-pressure against the straps – the heels, however, remaining firm – than he could make bricks without straw. The straps, in fact, are a most valuable aid to the recovery. Take them away from a crew and you will see one of two things: either the men will never swing nearly even to the upright position, and will recover with toil and trouble, or, if they swing back properly, they will all fall over backwards with their feet in the air. This slight strap-pressure just helps them over the difficult part of the recovery; as the body swings forward the feet immediately resume their balance against the stretcher. Indeed, if these movements are properly performed, you get a very pretty play of the toes and the ball of the foot against the stretcher, you counteract the tendency of the body to tumble forward, and you materially help the beginning from that part of the foot in which the spring resides. Totally to forbid men to use their straps seems to me a piece of pedantry. On this point I may fortify myself with the opinion of Mr W. B. Woodgate, as given in his *Badminton Book on Boating*. I am glad, too, to find that Mr S. Le Blanc Smith, of the London Rowing Club, a most finished and beautiful oarsman, whose record of victories at Henley is a sufficient testimony to his knowledge and skill, agrees with me. In an article published during a recent rowing controversy, he remarks, 'I think Mr — will find that all men, consciously or unconsciously, use the foot

strap more or less, to aid them in the first inch or two of recovery. If he doubts this, let him remove the strap and watch results, be the oarsman who he may.' I need only add that this pressure should never be greater than will just suffice to help the body recovery. If exaggerated, its result on slides will be to spoil swing by pulling the slide forward in advance of the body.

I have now, I think, taken you through all the complicated movements of the stroke, and there for the present I must leave you to carry out as best you can instructions which I have endeavoured to make as clear on paper as the difficulties of the subject permit. But I may be allowed to add a warning. Book reading may be a help; but rowing, like any other exercise, can only be properly learnt by constant and patient practice in boats under the eyes of competent instructors. Do not be discouraged because your improvement is slow, and because you are continually being rated for the same faults. With a slight amount of intelligence and a large amount of perseverance and good temper, these faults will gradually disappear, and as your limbs and muscles accustom themselves to the work, you will be moulded into the form of a skilled oarsman. Even the dread being who may be coaching you – winner of the Grand Challenge Cup or stroke-oar of his university though he be – had his crude and shapeless beginnings. He has passed through the mill, and now is great and glorious. But if you imagine that even he is faultless, just watch him as he rows, and listen to the remarks that a fearless and uncompromising coach permits himself to address to him. And to show you that others have suffered and misunderstood and have been misunderstood like yourself, I will wind up this chapter with 'The Wail of the Tubbed,' the lyrical complaint of some Cambridge rowing freshmen.

Sir, – We feel we are intruding, but we deprecate your blame,
We may plead our youth and innocence as giving us a claim;
We should blindly grope unaided in our efforts to do right,
So we look to you with confidence to make our darkness light.

We are freshmen – rowing freshmen; we have joined our
college club,
And are getting quite accustomed to our daily dose of tub;
We have all of us bought uniforms, white, brown, or blue, or red,
We talk rowing shop the livelong day, and dream of it in bed.

We sit upon our lexicons as 'Happy as a King'
(We refer you to the picture), and we practise how to swing;
We go every day to chapel, we are never, never late,
And we exercise our backs when there, and always keep
them straight.

We shoot our hands away – on land – as quick as any ball:
Balls always shoot, they tell us, when rebounding from a wall.
We decline the noun 'a bucket,' and should deem it – well,
a bore,
If we 'met,' when mainly occupied in oarsmanship, our oar.

But still there are a few things that our verdant little band,
Though we use our best endeavours, cannot fully understand.
So forgive us if we ask you, sir – we're dull, perhaps, but keen –
To explain these solemn mysteries and tell us what they mean.

For instance, we have heard a coach say, 'Five, you're
very rank;
Mind those eyes of yours, they're straying, always straying, on
the bank.'
We are not prone to wonder, but we looked with some surprise
At the owner of those strangely circumambulating eyes.

There's a stroke who 'slices awfully,' and learns without
remorse
That his crew are all to pieces at the finish of the course;
There's A., who 'chucks his head about,' and B., who 'twists and
screws,'
Like an animated gimlet in a pair of shorts and shoes.

And C. is 'all beginning,' so remark his candid friends;
It must wear him out in time, we think, this stroke that never
ends.
And though D. has no beginning, yet his finish is A1;
How can that possess a finish which has never been begun?

And E. apparently would be an oar beyond compare,
If the air were only water and the water only air.
And F., whose style is lofty, doubtless has his reasons why
He should wish to scrape the judgment seat, when rowing,
from the sky.

Then G. is far too neat for work, and H. is far too rough;
There's J., who lugs, they say, too much, and K. not half enough;
There's L., who's never fairly done, and M., who's done too
brown,
And N., who can't stand training, and poor O., who can't sit
down.

And P. is much too limp to last; there's Q. too stiffly starched;
And R., poor fool, whose inside wrist is never 'nicely arched.'
And, oh, sir, if you pity us, pray tell us, if you please,
What is meant by 'keep your button up,' and 'flatten down your
knees.'

'If an oar may be described as 'he,' there's no death half
so grim
As the death like which we hang on with our outside hands to
'him;'
But in spite of all our efforts, we have never grasped, have you?
How not to use 'those arms' of ours, and yet to pull it through.

S. 'never pulled his shoestrings.' If a man must pull at all,
Why uselessly pull shoestrings? Such a task would surely pall.
But T.'s offence is worse than that, he'll never get his Blue,
He thinks rowing is a pastime—well, we own we thought so too.

Then V.'s 'a shocking sugarer,' how bitter to be that!
X. flourishes his oar about as if it were a bat;
And Y. should be provided, we imagine, with a spade,
Since he always 'digs,' instead of 'merely covering his blade.'

Lastly, Z.'s a 'real old corker,' who will never learn to work,
For he puts his oar in gently and extracts it with a jerk.
Oh! Never has there been, we trow, since wickedness began,
Such a mass of imperfections as the perfect rowing man.

P.S. by Two Cynics.

So they coach us and reproach us (like a flock of silly jays
Taught by parrots how to feather) through these dull October
days.
We shall never understand them, so we shouldn't care a dam
If they all were sunk in silence at the bottom of the Cam.

No. 1. – Position at beginning of stroke. (This is a stationary photograph. In the movement of the swing the body will come still further down.)

No. 2. – Position just after catching, beginning. (Instantaneous Photograph.)

No. 3. – Position on halfway through stroke. (Stationary
Photograph.)

No. 4. – Position as arms are bending for finish. (Instantaneous
Photograph.)

No. 5 – The finish. (Stationary Photograph. In movement the body would go a little further back.)

First Lessons on Sliding Seats

Let me assume (I am still addressing my imaginary novice) that you have passed through the first few stages of your novitiate. If you are an Oxford or a Cambridge freshman you will have been carefully drilled in a tub pair, promoted later to a freshmen's four or eight, and during the next term may have been included in the Torpid or Lent Boat of your college. At any rate, I am assuming that you have by now rowed in a race or a series of races for eight-oared crews on fixed seats. But I prefer to leave the general subject of combined rowing, whether in eights or fours, to a later chapter, while I attempt to explain the mysteries and difficulties of the sliding seat.

The slide may be described as a contrivance for increasing the length of the stroke (i.e. of the period during which, the oar blade remaining covered in the water, power is applied to the propulsion of the boat), and for giving greater effect to the driving force of the oarsman's legs. Long before the actual sliding seat had been invented professional oarsmen and scullers had discovered that if they slid on their fixed thwarts they increased the pace of their boats, and even among amateurs this practice was not unknown. Mr R. H. Labat has told me that so far back as 1870 he and his colleagues fitted their rowing trousers with leather, greased their thwarts, and so slid on them. In 1872 slides were used at Henley Regatta, and in 1873 the Oxford and Cambridge crews for the first time rowed their race on slides, Cambridge winning in 19 minutes 35 seconds, which remained as record time until 1892. This performance, though it was undoubtedly helped by good conditions of tide and wind, served to establish slides firmly in popular favour, and from that time onwards fixed seats were practically retained only for the coaching of novices and, in eights, for the Torpids and Lent Races at Oxford and Cambridge. Now, proceeding on the principle that rowing is meant to be an exercise of grace, symmetry, and skill, as well as of strength and endurance, I think I may lay it down as an essential rule that it is necessary on slides to observe those instructions which made fixed-seat rowing in the old days a pleasure to the eye. In the very early days of slides, while men were still groping for correct principles, this important axiom was too often neglected. It was imagined that swing was no longer necessary, and accordingly the rivers were filled with contorted oarsmen shuffling and tumbling and screwing on their slides. Veteran oars and coaches, to whom 'form' was as the apple of their eye, were horror-struck, and gave vent to loud lamentations, utterly condemning this horrible innovation, which, as they thought, had reduced oarsmanship to the level of a rough and tumble fight. 'If both Universities,' wrote the Revd A. T. W. Shadwell in his 'Notes on Boat-building,' published in the *Record of the University Boat Race* in 1881,

> would condescend to ask Dr. Warre to construct for them, and if their crews would also either learn to use the sliding apparatus effectively, or to discard it as pernicious and as an enemy to real oarsmanship when not thoroughly mastered, then we should be treated again to the welcome spectacle of boats travelling instead of dragging, riding over the water instead of the water washing over the canvas, combined with that still more-to-be-desired spectacle of faultless form and faultless time—eight men ground into one perfect machine. Nothing short of that result will satisfy those who know what eight-oared rowing ought to be, and lament its decadence.

Yet Cambridge had produced the 1876 crew, Oxford the 1878 crew, both of them models of style, unison and strength, and Leander both in 1875 and in 1880 had won the Grand Challenge Cup with admirable crews composed exclusively of university men. It would seem, therefore, as if Mr Shadwell's strictures were undeserved, at least by the better class of university oars. The fact is that by that time, and for some years before that time, the true principles of sliding had been acquired, and the more serious defects of form had once more become the cherished possession of inferior college crews. But then, even in the glorious old fixed-seat days, college crews were not always remarkable for the beauty and correctness of their form. I am not going to deny that the difficulty of teaching good style has been increased by the addition of the sliding seat; but there have been innumerable examples during the last quarter of a century to prove that this difficulty can be faced and entirely overcome. Four crews I have already mentioned. I may add to them, not as exhausting the list of good crews, but as being splendid examples of combined style and power, the London Rowing Club crew of 1881, which won the final of the Grand from the outside station against Leander and Twickenham; the Oxford crews of 1892, 1896 and 1897; the crews of Trinity Hall, the Oxford Etonians, and the Thames Rowing Club in 1886 and 1887; the Cambridge crew and the Thames Rowing Club crew of 1888; the London Rowing Club crew of 1890; the Leander crews of 1891, 1893, 1894 and 1896; and the New College and Leander crews of the present year. It is fortunate that this should be so, for, the proof of the pudding being in the eating, it is hardly likely that crews will abandon a device which, while it has actually increased pace over the Henley course by close on half a minute, has rendered skill and watermanship of higher value, and has given an additional effect to physical strength.

During my undergraduate days at Cambridge, and for some years afterwards (say, up to about 1884), the slide tracks in racing boats were sixteen inches long. This, allowing seven inches as the breadth of the seat itself, would give the slide a 'play,' or movement, of nine inches. The front stop, which forms the limit of the forward movement of the slide, was fixed so as to bring the front edge of the slide to a point five inches from the 'work,' i.e. from a line drawn straight across the boat from the back, or rowing, thole. At the finish of the stroke, therefore, when the slide had been driven full back, its front edge was fourteen inches away from the work. To put it in technical language, we slid up to five inches from our work and finished fourteen inches away from it. Since that time slides have become longer, and there are but few racing boats in which the slide-tracks are less than twenty-two or even twenty-three inches long, giving the slide a play of fifteen or sixteen inches. The front edge of the slide now moves forward (when I say 'forward' I speak in relation to the movement of the body and not in relation to the ends of the boat) to a point which is level with the work. In other words, we now slide up to our work and finish fifteen or sixteen inches from it. On these long slides, when the body has attained the full reach, the flanks are closed in upon the thighs, the knees are bent until the thighs come fairly close to the calves, and, ex-necessario, the ankle joints are very much bent. It is plain that great flexibility of hip joints, knees, and ankles must be attained in order that the slide may be used fully up to the last fraction of an inch in coming forward. This flexibility very few novices, and not all old stagers, possess. The muscles and joints at first absolutely refuse to accommodate themselves to this new strain, and you will see a man as he slides forward, taking his heels well off the stretcher in order to ease the strain upon his ankles, and moving his shoulders back long before his oar has gripped the water in order to relieve his hip joints. This results in his missing the whole of his beginning, striking the water at right-angles to his rigger instead of well behind it, and having absolutely no firmness of drive when it becomes necessary for him to use his legs. In order, therefore, that matters may be made easier for novices, and that they may be brought on gradually, I strongly advise coaches to start them on slides much shorter than those now in vogue. A slide with a play of eight inches, coming to a point six inches from the work, is ample. A few days will make a wonderful difference, and later on, when the first stiffness has worn off and the movements have become easier, the slide can be gradually increased. At Oxford and Cambridge the proper seasons for such preliminary practice would be the Lent Term, when Torpids and Lent Races are over, and the beginning of the October term, when many College clubs – at any rate at Cambridge – organize Sliding-seat Trial Eights in clinker-built boats.

Two further points remain to be noticed. On fixed seats the ankles hardly bend up as the body swings forward, and it is possible, therefore, to use a stretcher fixed almost erect in the boat, the seat being placed eleven or twelve inches from the work. But with slides, as I have explained, the seat moves to a point which in racing boats is now level with the work, and few ankles are capable of submitting to the strain which would be involved if the stretchers were set up as erect ('proud' is the technical term) as they are with fixed seats. It is necessary, therefore, to set the stretchers more off on an incline (technically, to 'rake' them). It will be found, I think, that, assuming a stretcher to be one foot in height, a set-off of nine inches will be amply sufficient for most novices, even on full slides. I have myself never found any difficulty in maintaining my feet firm on a stretcher of this rake or even of less, and I have known some very supple-jointed men, e.g. Mr H. Willis, of the Leander Crews of 1896 and 1897, who preferred to row with a stretcher set up a good deal prouder. But the average oar is not very supple-jointed, though his facility in this respect can be greatly improved by practice. To make things easier – and after all our object should be to smooth away all the oarsman's external difficulties – I consider it advisable to fix heel-traps to the stretcher. This simple device, by the pressure which it exercises against the back of the heels, counteracts their tendency to come away from the stretcher; but even with heel-traps, I have seen stiff-jointed oarsmen make the most superbly successful efforts to bring their heels away.

The second point is this: With sliding seats you require an oar of longer leverage (i.e. inboard measurement from rowing-face of button to end of handle) than with fixed seats. For a fixed seat an oar with a leverage of 3 feet 5½ inches should suffice. With long slides the leverage of an oar should not be less than 3 feet 8 inches, nor more than 3 feet 8½ inches. For this I assume that the distance of the centre of the seat from the sill of the row-lock is 2 feet 7 inches. With regard to leverage, there is a practical unanimity of opinion among modern oarsmen. With regard to the outboard measurement of oars and the proper width of blade, they differ somewhat, but I can reserve this matter for the next chapter, merely premising that in any case it is not advisable to start your novices in gigs with oar blades broader than 5¾ inches.

Let me imagine, then, that my pupil is seated in the gig, his stretcher having been fixed at a point that will enable him, when his slide is full back, and he is sitting on it easily without pressing, to have his knees slightly bent.

And now to the business of instruction –

1. Remember and endeavour to apply all the lessons you have learnt on fixed seats. Slides add another element to the stroke. They do not alter the elements you have previously been taught.

    Beginning. – Get hold of this just as you would on a fixed seat, with a sharp spring of the whole body, which thus begins its swing back without the loss of a fraction of time.

    (a) The natural tendency of a tiro will be to drive his slide away before his shoulders have begun to move. This must at all costs be avoided. In order to secure the effectual combination of body swing and legwork, it is essential that the swing should start first.

    (b) It is equally reprehensible to swing the body full back before starting the slide; you thus cut the stroke into two distinct parts, one composed of mere body swing, the other of mere legwork.

Therefore:

2. When the body-swing backwards has started, but only the smallest fractional part of a second afterwards – so quickly, indeed, as to appear to the eye of a spectator almost a simultaneous movement – let the slide begin to travel back, the swing meanwhile continuing.

   (a) Remember what was said in fixed-seat instructions as to the use of the toes and the ball of the foot at the beginning of the stroke. On slides this is even more important.

3. Body and slide are now moving back in unison, the feet pressing with firm and steady pressure against the stretcher, and the arms perfectly straight. As the slide moves, the leg power applied must on no account diminish. If anything it ought to increase, for the body is beginning to lose its impetus, and the main part of the resistance is transferred to the legs, the blade all the time moving at an even pace through the water.

4. The body must swing a little further back than on a fixed seat.

5. Body swing and slide back should end at the same moment.

6. As they end, the knees should be pressed firmly down so as to enable you to secure the last ounce of leg power from the stretcher. Simultaneously with this depression of the legs, the hands (and particularly the outside hand, which has been doing the main share of the work of the stroke all through) must bring the oar handle firmly home to the chest, sweeping it in and thus obtaining what is called a firm hard finish. As the knees come finally down, the elbows pass the sides, and the shoulders move back and downwards.

   (a) Mr W. B. Woodgate, in the *Badminton Book on Boating*, says:

   Many good oarsmen slide until the knees are quite straight. In the writer's opinion this is waste of power: the knees should never quite straighten; the recovery is, for anatomical reasons, much stronger if the joint is slightly bent when the reversal of the machinery commences. The extra half-inch of kick gained by quite straightening the knees hardly compensates for the extra strain of recovery; also leg-work to the last fraction of a second of swing is better preserved by this retention of a slight bend, and an open chest and clean finish are thereby better attained.

If Mr Woodgate means that the legs are not to be pressed down as the stroke finishes, but are to remain loosely bent, I differ from him, though, considering his high authority, with hesitation and regret. As a matter of fact, the front edge of the thwart catches the calves of the legs at the finish, when the legs are pressed down, and prevents the knees from being absolutely straightened. But I am certain that unless an oarsman assures his legs in the firm position that I have explained, he will lose most valuable power at the end of the stroke, and will materially increase his difficulty in taking his oar clean out of the water and generally in getting a smart recovery. This final leg pressure not only supports the body in a somewhat trying position, but enables the hands to come home to the chest without faltering. As on fixed seats, it is essential that the body should not be pulled forward to meet the oar. And it is equally essential that it should not sink down or fall away from the hands, thus rendering an elastic recovery impossible.

> (b) The blade, as on fixed seats, must be kept fully covered to the finish, and there must be power on it to the last fraction of an inch. If a man takes his oar out of the water before he has fairly ended his stroke, and rows his finish in the air, or if he partially uncovers his blade and rows 'light,' he commits in either case a serious fault. In the former case his whole bodyweight, which ought to be propelling the boat, not only ceases to have any good effect, but becomes so much dead lumber, and actually impedes her progress. In the latter he can only exert half, or, it may be, one quarter of his proper power during an appreciable part of the stroke.

7. The drop of the hands, the turn of the wrists, the shootout of the hands, and the straightening of the arms must be performed precisely as on a fixed seat, but the legs, meanwhile, are to remain braced, so that knees may not hamper hands. As soon as ever the hands have been shot out, and immediately after the start of the forward swing, the slide comes into play, and the knees consequently begin to bend outwards and upwards. It is very important not to pause or 'hang' on the recovery.

8. The recovery movements ought to release the body smartly, but care must be taken not to hustle the body forward with a rush before the arms are straightened. The body begins to swing from the hips as soon as the hands release it, but the swing is to be a slow one.

    (a) Do not begin to slide forward before you swing. Let your swing just have the precedence, and let it then carry your slide with it.

9. The pace of the swing forward must be slow and unvarying, and the slide, therefore, must also move slowly. The time occupied by the swing should be the body's rest.

10. Remember the fixed-seat instructions as to balance against the stretcher with the feet during the swing forward, and especially during the latter part of it. The fault of tumbling forward over the stretcher is far too common, and can only be avoided or corrected by maintaining the pressure on the stretcher. In fact, never let your body get out of control. You ought to feel and to look as if at any moment during the swing forward you could stop dead at the word of command. Swing and slide should practically end together, the body 'snaking out,' as I have heard it expressed, in the final part of the swing, but without 'pecking' over the front-stop. There must be no overreach with the shoulders.

11. When the body is full forward the knees should be opened to about the breadth of the armpits, the flanks closed in against the thighs. The knees should bend steadily and gradually into this position, and at the moment of beginning they must maintain themselves there and not fall loosely apart. Such a movement entails a great loss of power at the beginning of the next stroke. Nor, on the other hand, ought the knees to be clipped together as the stroke begins.

12. Remember, finally, that grace, erectness, straightness of back and arms, and a clean precision, balance and elasticity of all movements are as important now as they were on fixed seats. A man who on slides rounds his back, humps up his shoulders, and hollows his chest may do good work, but it will be in spite of and not because of these serious disfigurements. Only by carefully observing fixed rules and by prolonged practice will you be able to attain to the harmonious ease and elegance by which a comparatively weak man can so economize his strength as to outrow and outlast some brawny giant who wastes his power in useless contortions.

Combined Oarsmanship In Eights

The novice, having passed successfully through his period of apprenticeship, is by this time ready, let us suppose, to be included in an eight-oared, sliding-seat crew, either for his college or for the rowing club to which he may happen to belong. He will marvel at first at the fragile and delicate fabric of the craft in which he is asked to take his place. One-eighth of an inch of cedar divides him from the waters that are to be the scene of his prowess. In stepping into the boat he must exercise the greatest care. The waterman and the coxswain are firmly holding the riggers, while the oarsman, placing a hand on each gunwale to support himself, steps cautiously with one foot on to the kelson, or backbone of the ship. Then he seats himself upon his slide, fits his feet into the stretcher-straps, and inserts his oar in the rowlock, finally getting the button into its proper place by raising the handle, and so working at it until the button comes in under the string that passes from thole to thole, and keeps the oar from flying out of the rowlock. His seven companions having performed the same feats, the boat is now shoved out from the bank, and the work of the day begins.

The oarsman who thus takes his first voyage in a racing-ship, built, as all racing ships are, without a keel, must remember that her stability, when she contains her crew, is obtained merely by the balance of the oars. Remove the oars, and the boat would immediately roll over to one side or the other, and immerse her crew in the water. With eight bodies and oars in a constant state of movement, the problem of keeping the boat upon an even keel is not an easy one. It can only be solved satisfactorily in one way: there must be absolute harmony in every movement. The hands must come in and out at the same moment and at the same level, and the oar blades must necessarily be maintained, on the feather and throughout the swing, at the uniform level prescribed for them by the harmonious movement of eight pairs of hands. The bodies must begin, continue, and end the swing together; the blades must strike the water at precisely the same moment; all the bodies must swing back as if released from one spring; the slides must move together; the arms bend as by one simultaneous impulse; and the eight oar blades, having swept through the water in a uniform plane, must leave it as though they were part of a single machine, and not moved by eight independent wills. When this unison of movements has been attained by long and persevering practice, marred by frequent periods of disappointment, by knuckles barked as the boat rolls and the hands scrape along the gunwale, and by douches of cold water as the oars splash, then, and not till then, may it be said that a crew has got together.

The above details concern the harmony and unison of the crew. It is obvious, however, that the eight men who compose it may be harmonized into almost any kind of style, and it is important, therefore, to settle what is the best style which will secure the greatest possible pace at the smallest cost of effort. In the first place, then, you must remember and endeavour to apply all the instructions I have laid down in the two previous chapters. These were framed upon the supposition that you were trying to qualify yourself to row eventually in a light racing ship. Summing these up generally, and without insisting again upon details, I may say that you are required to have a long, steady, and far-reaching body swing; you must grip the beginning of the stroke well behind the rigger at the full reach forward without the loss of a fraction of a second, with a vigorous spring back of the whole body, so as to apply the bodyweight immediately to the blade of the oar. As your body swings back, your feet are to press against the stretcher and drive the slide back, in order that, by the combination of body swing and leg drive, you may retain the power which you have applied at the beginning evenly throughout the whole of the stroke. It is essential that the body should not fall away at the finish, but maintain an easy, graceful position, so that, with a final pressure of the legs, the swing of the elbows past the sides, and a rowing back of the shoulders which opens the chest, the hands may be swept fair and square home, the oar blade being meanwhile covered, but not more than covered, from the moment it enters the water until it is taken clean out. The hands must then leave the chest as a billiard ball rebounds from the cushion, in order that you may have a smart and elastic recovery. This swift motion of the hands straightens the arms, and releases the body for its forward swing. The body swing forward, as I cannot too often repeat, must be slow, especially during its latter part; in fact, during that swing, a perfect balance must be maintained, the feet being well planted against the stretcher. When a man rows in this style with seven other men, in absolute time and harmony with them, he will find a rhythmical pleasure and a delightful ease in movements which at the outset were cramped and difficult. Then, as he swings his body, grips the water and drives his swirling oar blade through, he will feel that every ounce of strength he puts forth has its direct and appreciable influence upon the pace of the boat. Not for him then will it be to envy the bird in its flight, as, with all his muscles braced, his lungs clear, and his heart beating soundly, he helps to make his craft move like a thing of life over the water.

That is the ideal. Let us come down to the actual. I will imagine myself to be coaching an average crew in a racing ship.

I must first of all assure myself that the boat is properly rigged, and that the men have a fair chance of rowing with comfort. The thole pins should stand absolutely straight from the sill of the rowlock. If the rowing pin is bent outwards towards the water in the slightest degree, the oar will have a tendency to 'slice,' and a feather under water will be the result. The actual wood of the rowing pin, however, should be slightly filed away at the bottom, so as to incline a very, very little towards the stern of the boat. Care must be taken also to have a sufficient width between the thole pins to prevent the oar from locking on the full reach. The rowlock strings must be taut. They must have a sufficient pressure on the oar to prevent the button being forced out of the rowlock. For these and other details, the table of measurements given at the end of this chapter should be consulted.

In this crew I will suppose that five of the members have already had experience in lightship rowing. The three others – bow, No. 3, and No. 4 – are quite new to the game. I point out to these three, to begin with, the importance of balancing the boat by having their arms rigidly straight as they swing forward, so as to be able, by the slightest amount of give and take from the shoulders, to counteract any tendency to roll, by sitting firmly on their seats, and not shifting about to right or to left, and by keeping their feet well on the stretchers. That done, the words of command will come from the cox. 'Get ready all!' (At this command, the oarsmen divest themselves of all unnecessary clothing.) 'Forward all!' (The oarsmen swing and slide forward to within about two-thirds of the full-reach position, the backs of the blades lying flat upon the water.)

'Are you ready?' (This is merely a call to attention.) 'Paddle!' (At this the blades are turned over square, and immediately grip the water, and the boat starts.) During the progress of this imaginary crew, I propose to invest them individually and collectively with certain faults, and to offer suggestions for their improvement, just as if I were coaching them from the bank or from a steam-launch.

1. 'Stroke, you're tumbling forward over your stretcher. Keep the last part of your swing very slow by balancing against the stretcher with your feet as you swing forward. That's better. You got a beginning twice as hard that time.'

2. 'Seven, you're feathering under water. Keep pressure on to the very finish of the stroke, and drop your hands a little more, so as to get the oar out square and clean. Use the legs well at the finish.'

3. 'Six, you're very slow with your hands. Consequently, your body rushes forward to make up for lost time. Shoot the hands away quickly, with a sharp turn of the inside wrist. Then let the body follow slowly.'

4. 'Five, you slide too soon and fall away from your oar at the finish. Get your shoulders and the whole of your bodyweight well on to the beginning, so as to start swinging back before you drive your slide away. At the finish keep your shoulders down and sit up well upon your bones.'

5. 'Four and three, your blades are coming out of the water long before any of the others. This is because you are afraid of reaching properly forward. You therefore get your oars in scarcely if at all behind the rigger, and consequently there is not enough resistance to your oar in the water to enable you to hold out the stroke fully to the finish. Swing, and reach well forward, and let your oars strike the beginning at the point to which your reach has brought it. You may splash at first, but with a little confidence you will soon get over that. Three, you're late. As you come forward you press heavily on the handle of your oar, the blade soars up, and is coming down through the air when the rest have struck the water. Keep your hands, especially the inside one, light on the handle of the oar, and let them come up as the body swings forward.'

6. 'Two, your arms are bending too soon. Try to swing back with perfectly straight arms. Don't imagine that you can row your stroke merely by the power of your arms. Also try and keep your shoulders down at the finish and on the recovery.'

7. 'Bow, swing back straight. Your body is falling out of the boat at the finish. Use the outside leg and hand more firmly through the stroke, and row the hands a little higher in to the chest; also arch the inside of the wrist a little more to help you in turning the oar on the feather.'

So much for individuals. Now for the crew.

1. 'The finish and recovery are not a bit together. I can almost hear eight distinct sounds as the oars turn in the rowlocks. Try and lock it up absolutely together. There ought to be a sound like the turning of a key in a well-oiled lock—sharp, single, and definite.'

(Note. – This is a very important point. On the unison with which the wrists turn and the hands shoot away depends the unison of the next stroke. When once, in coaching, you have locked your crew together on this point, you will greatly decrease the difficulty of the rest of your task.)

2. 'Don't let the boat roll down on the bow oars. Stroke side, catch the beginning a little sharper. Bow side, when the roll of the boat begins, do not give in to it by still further lowering your hands. Keep your hands up.' (The same instruction applies, mutatis mutandis, when the boat rolls on the stroke oars. Apart from individual eccentricities, a boat is often brought down on the one bank of oars by the fact that the opposite side, or one or two of them, grip the water a little too late.)

3. 'You are all of you slow with your hands. Rattle them out sharply, and make your recovery much more lively. Steady now! Don't rush forward. Keep the swing slow and long. You are all much too short on the swing, and consequently get no length in the water.'

4. 'Watch the bodies in front of you as they move, and mould yourself on their movement.'

5. 'You have fallen to pieces again. Use your ears as well as your eyes, and listen for the rattle of the oars in the rowlocks. Whenever you fall to pieces, try to rally on that point. Also plant your feet firmly on the stretchers, and use your legs more when the boat rolls.'

These, I think, are a fair sample of the faults that may be found in almost any crew, and to their eradication coach and oarsmen have patiently to devote themselves.

Snapshot of a crew in motion.

MEASUREMENTS OF AN EIGHTOARED RACING BOAT

For purposes of convenience, I have taken the following measurements from a boat built by Rough for Leander, in 1891. In that year she carried a very heavy crew, who won the Grand Challenge Cup at Henley in record time. She repeated her Grand Challenge victory in 1892 and 1893, with crews very differently constituted from the first one: –

(1) Length over all 60 feet 3 inches
(2) Beam amidships, under gunwale 1 feet 11 inches
(3) Depth amidships, under gunwale 1 feet 1 inch
(4) Height of thwarts above skin of boat 0 feet 7⅛ inches
(5) Height of seats above skin of boat 0 feet 9⅛ inches
(6) Height of rowlock sills above seat 0 feet 6⅞ inches
(7) Height of heels above skin of boat 0 feet 1¼ inches
(8) Position of front edge of slide in relation to rowing pin when well forward level
(9) Length of movement of slide 1 feet 4 inches
(10) Distance from rowing-pin, measured horizontally and at right angles to boat, to centre of seat 2 feet 7 inches
(11) Distance from wood of one thole-pin to wood of the other 0 feet 4⅞ inches

This boat, like nearly all English Eights, was 'side seated,' i.e. the centre of the seat, instead of being over the kelson, was set away from it, and from the outrigger. Bow's and stroke's seats were 2½ inches from centre, No. 5's 3½ inches. Nearly all Fours and Pairs in England are now centre seated, as are Eights in America. Of course, with centre seating, assuming that you want the same leverage, you require a longer outrigger. Otherwise, the only difference between the two systems would seem to be that with centre seating you naturally align the bodies better.

Since 1891 boatbuilders have somewhat increased the length of the boats they build, and it is not uncommon now to find boats with a measurement of 63 feet and a few inches over all. The boat whose measurements I have given had, if I remember rightly, a slightly wider beam at No. 3 stretcher than she had amidships. I have noticed, and my experience in this respect confirms that of Mr W. B. Woodgate, though it is entirely opposed to the Revd A. T. Shadwell's theories, that a boat with a full beam somewhere between No. 4 and No. 3 is always a fast one. A boat should never dip her head, but should always maintain it free.

MEASUREMENT OF OARS

On this matter there is now a great divergence of opinion among rowing men. From 1891 inclusive up to the present year, the Leander crews have, with trifling divergences, rowed with oars built on the following measurements:—

(1) Length over all 12 feet
(2) Length in-board, i.e. measured from rowing face of bottom to end of handle 3 feet 8 inches

[NB. In some cases an extra half-inch was added, which would make the length over all 12 feet ½ inch]

(3) Length of button from top to bottom, measured in a straight line 0 feet 3¼ inches
(4) Length of blade measured over the arc of the scoop 2 feet 7 inches
(5) Breadth of blade 0 feet 6 inches

[NB. These are what are called square blades, i.e. the widest part came at the end. Barrel blades are those in which the widest part comes about the middle. In 1893 an extra half-inch was added outboard. In 1896 the length of the Leander oars over all was only 11 feet 11⅛ inches, the inboard measurement being 3 feet 8 inches. With these oars the Leander crew defeated Yale, and in the next heat, after a very severe struggle, rowed down and defeated New College, who were rowing with oars three inches longer outboard. Here are the measurements of the oars with which the Eton crew won the Ladies' Plate in 1885 –

Over all 12 feet 6 inches
Inboard 3 feet 7½ inches
Length of blade 2 feet 5 inches
Breadth of blade near shank 0 feet 6⅜ inches
Breadth of blade at end 0 feet 5 inches
(These blades were coffin shaped on a pattern invented by Dr. Warre.)

Measurement of Oars of Oxford Crew, 1890.
Over all 12 feet 3⅛ inches
Inboard 3 feet 8½ inches
Length of blade 2 feet 7 inches
Greatest breadth 0 feet 6½ inches
(These were barrel blades.)

In 1896 the Oxford crew rowed with oars measuring 12 feet 2 inches over all, with a leverage of 3 feet 8¼ inches, and blade 6 inches broad. With these, it will be remembered, they rowed down and defeated Cambridge, after a magnificent struggle, by two-fifths of a length, Cambridge using oars measuring some 3 inches longer outboard. It will thus be seen that short oars have a very good record to support them – especially over the Henley course. This year, however, a reaction took place at Oxford in favour of longer oars with narrower blades. The Oxford Eight of this year rowed with oars measuring 12 feet 6 inches over all, the extra length being, of course, outboard, and their blades were cut down to a breadth of 5½ inches. They were, by common consent, a very fine crew, but were unable to command a fast rate of stroke, and in the race against an inferior crew they hardly did themselves or their reputation justice. This pattern of oar was used by New College at Henley, the blades, however, being further cut down to 5¼ inches. In the final heat of the Grand Challenge Cup, they met Leander, who were rowing with 12 feet oars. Leander, rowing a considerably faster stroke, at once jumped ahead, and led by a length in three minutes. New College, however, came up to them, still rowing a slower stroke, then picked their stroke up, and, after rowing level with Leander for about 250 yards, finally defeated them by 2 feet. The result of this race cannot be said to have settled the question as between long oars and short. In the Stewards' Fours, on the other hand, Leander, rowing with oars measuring 12 feet ½ inch over all, and blades 5¾ inches in breadth, defeated New College, rowing with 12 feet 6 inches oars, and blades of 5½ inches, the leverage in both cases being 3 feet 8½ inches. The advocates of the long oar maintain that they secure a longer stride, and are thus able to economize strength by using a slower rate of stroke.

Those who favour the shorter ones believe that the extra lightness of their implement enables them to row a faster stroke without unduly tiring themselves. Personally, I found, after trying the experiment several times, that Leander crews I have coached invariably rowed better and commanded more speed in practice with 12 feet to 12 feet 1 inch oars than with oars 3 inches or 4 inches longer.

It must be remembered, finally, that men, as well as measurements, have something to do with the pace of a crew, and that style and uniformity count for a good deal. The advocates of long or short oars will always be able to explain a defeat sustained by one of their crews by alleging causes that are totally unconnected with the measurement of the oars. On the other hand, such is their enthusiasm, they will attribute the victory of their crew entirely to their favourite pattern of oar.

Combined Oarsmanship in Eights (continued)

Now that the novice has been safely launched in his racing ship, we may hark back for a space and consider some important points connected with the organization and management of an eight-oared crew. And first as to its selection and arrangement.

As a general rule, it may be laid down that two middleweights (men ranging from 11 stone 5 lbs. to 11 stone 10 lbs or even to 12 stone) will be best at stroke and No. 7; three heavyweights (12 stone 4 lbs and upwards) will suit for No. 6, No. 5, and No. 4; then with two more middleweights at No. 3 and No. 2, and a lightweight (10 stone to 11 stone 3 lbs or so) at bow, your crew will be complete. This sounds easy enough, but in practice the matter is complicated by a hundred difficulties, such as (a) a superfluity or (b) a total absence of good heavyweights; (c) the absence of any good middleweights possessing the peculiar qualities necessary for stroke and No. 7; and (d) the inability of good oars to row on one side or the other of the boat, for you may find that of six valuable oars whom you may want to include in a crew, everyone will tell you that he can only row on the stroke side or the bow side, as the case may be. In theory, of course, every man ought to be able to row equally well on both sides. In practice it will be found that most men, apart from any conscious preference on their own part, do better work on one side than on the other, while some are absolutely useless if shifted from the side they prefer. This last class is, however, not nearly so numerous as it used to be; and if, for instance, you consult the list of victorious Oxford crews from 1890 up to the present year, and compare it further with lists of Leander crews and Oxford College crews, you will see that a very large number of men have rowed and won races on both sides of the boat. I may mention specially Mr Guy Nickalls, Mr C. W. Kent, Mr W. A. L. Fletcher, Mr R. P. P. Rowe, Mr W. F. C. Holland, Mr H. B. Cotton, Mr M. C. Pilkington,

Mr C. D. Burnell, Mr T. H. E. Stretch, Mr C. K. Philips, Mr C. M. Pitman, and Mr H. G. Gold. On the other hand, I cannot remember – to take only two instances of excellent heavies – that Mr E. G. Tew or Mr W. Burton Stewart ever rowed except on the bow side.

All such difficulties the captain and coach of a crew must overcome as best they can. In any case they will find it advisable to put their lighter men in the stern and the bows, dumping down their heavies in the waist of the boat, where they will have more room, and where it will be easier to correct the clumsiness which is often associated with great weight.

STROKE

For stroke I like a man of not more than twelve stone. A few good strokes, e.g. the late Mr J. H. D. Goldie, have topped this weight by a few pounds. But a real heavyweight is almost invariably slow and lacking in initiative when placed at stroke, although, in the middle of the boat, with another man acting as fugleman for him, he may be able to row perfectly well at any rate of stroke that may be set to him. A long-backed, supple-jointed man is of course best, for the short-backed, long-legged man invariably has trouble in clearing his knees, and consequently develops faults of style which is hard to eradicate or even to reduce when he has no model in front of him. These faults will therefore exercise a very deleterious influence on the rest of the crew. As to temperament, I should select a good fighter, a man, that is, who would rather die than abandon the struggle, and whose fiery determined nature does not exclude perfect coolness and mastery over himself when a crisis calls for resource. Let me cite some examples.

I may begin my list with Mr H. P. Marriott and Mr C. D. Shafto, the Oxford and Cambridge strokes of 1877, the dead-heat year. It is rare indeed to find two such splendid performers matched against one another. Mr L. R. West, the Oxford stroke of 1880, 1881, and 1883, was as good a stroke as ever came to the university from Eton. He only weighed eleven stone, but his style was simply perfect. The finest demonstration of his racing judgment was given when he took his crew off at the start in 1883, and left Cambridge, on whom odds of three to one had been laid, struggling hopelessly in the rear. More familiarly known to me was the rowing of Mr F. I. Pitman. In the University Boat Race of 1886 both crews started at a very fast rate, and rowed little under thirty-eight to the minute all the way to Hammersmith Bridge, which was passed by Cambridge with a trifling lead. Immediately afterwards a strong head-wind and a rough sea were encountered; the rate of stroke in both boats dropped to about thirty-two, and Oxford began to forge steadily ahead, until at Barnes Bridge they led by nearly two lengths. Here the water was again smooth, and Mr F. I. Pitman, the Cambridge stroke, nerved himself for a supreme effort. With a wonderful spurt he picked it up, and in the first half-minute after Barnes, actually rowed twenty-one strokes, and in the full minute forty. The result of the race in favour of Cambridge is a matter of history; but, even had Cambridge lost, the merits of that wonderful spurt would have remained as striking.

MR C. W. KENT

Mr C. W. Kent, of Oxford and Leander fame, is another remarkable instance of a born stroke. He rarely rowed as much as eleven stone, and his general appearance outside a boat hardly gave promise of his marvellous vigour and endurance in a race. He is a loose-limbed, long-armed man, with no superfluous flesh, and with very little muscle. In any purely gymnastic competition he would stand no chance whatever. Yet it is not too much to say that as stroke of an Eight or a Four no man has ever been of greater value, none has a more brilliant record of victories secured by his own courage and resource after desperate struggles. He was not a very easy man to follow in the early stages of practice, but when once he had got his crew together behind him, he had the most absolute control over them, and could always get the last possible ounce of work out of them, and yet leave himself with sufficient vigour to wind them up to a final extra spurt if the necessity arose. His crew behind him became a single living entity, on which he could play as a musician plays on an instrument over which he has perfect command. He seemed to have a sort of intuitive knowledge, not merely of the capacity of his own crew, but also of the capacity of his opponents, at any given moment in a race. And he had, moreover, the gift – inestimably valuable in a stroke – of taking his men along at their best pace while economizing his own strength, thus always leaving himself with a margin to put in extra work and pace when a close finish required them. For there is no crew, however hard the men may have worked, and however greatly they may be exhausted, that cannot screw itself up to follow if only their stroke will give them a lead. Mr Kent's record of brilliant achievements begins in 1889, when, as stroke of the Brasenose crew, with Mr W. F. C. Holland at No. 7, he maintained his boat at the head of the river against the repeated attacks of a considerably stronger and faster New College crew. In 1890 he was stroke of a Brasenose four at Henley. In one of the preliminary heats of the Stewards' Cup, this crew defeated a strong Leander Four by two feet. In the final heat they had to meet the Thames Rowing Club. At Fawley Court, the halfway point, Thames had secured a lead of two lengths, and were apparently rowing well within themselves. From here, however, Mr Kent began an extraordinary series of spurts. With a relentless persistence, his crew rowing as one man behind him, he drove his boat inch by inch up to the Thames boat, drew level with them about 300 yards from the finish, and then, reinvigorated by the sight of his rivals, sailed past them and won the race by something more than a length. In 1891, as stroke of the Leander Eight he still further distinguished himself. Rowing from the unsheltered station against a strong 'Bushes' wind, he just managed by a final effort to avert defeat at the hands of the Thames Rowing Club, and made a dead heat of it. On the following day, there being no wind, Leander beat Thames by two lengths, and in the final heat beat the London Rowing Club by a length. Again, in the final heat of the Grand Challenge Cup in 1894, he won another terrible race from the worse station by half a length against the Thames Rowing Club. No one who saw that extraordinary race can forget the wonderful succession of efforts put forth both by Mr Kent and by the Thames stroke, Mr J. C. Gardner, a very fine and powerful oar, who had stroked Cambridge to victory in 1888 and 1889. Time after time did Mr Gardner force his boat almost level with Leander, and time after time Mr Kent just stalled him off and reasserted his crew's lead, until at the last he went in with horse, foot, and artillery, and won the furious contest. I cannot forbear citing another instance which shows merit as great, though of a different order, in this remarkable stroke. In 1891 he stroked the Oxford Eight, a crew of very heavy metal, but not well arranged, and containing one welterweight, who, in consequence of a severe attack of influenza during the earlier stages of training, could not be depended upon to last at top pressure over the whole of a course of four miles and a quarter. In fact, Oxford, considering their material, were unaccountably slow, and Cambridge, admirably stroked by Mr G. E. Elin, were as unaccountably fast. The race, it will be remembered, was a very close one, and was won by Oxford by only half a length. During its progress there were many temptations to Mr Kent, a man whose favourite rate of stroke was as a rule not less than forty, to increase the pace. He saw the Cambridge crew hanging doggedly on to him, and there were not wanting voices from his own crew to urge him to pick it up. But Mr Kent knew the capacity of his crew, and knew that, though a fast spurt might give him a temporary advantage, it would leave him in all probability with a completely exhausted heavyweight on his hands to struggle hopelessly against Cambridge's next effort. So he resolutely kept the stroke slow until he got to Chiswick, where he made his only effort, a slight one, it is true, but just sufficient to give him a margin on which he could win the race.

MR H. G. GOLD

I have dwelt at some length on Mr. Kent's performances, because I think that he showed in the highest degree all the qualities that make a man a good stroke in spite of the absence of mere brute strength. Mr C. M. Pitman, who as a freshman stroked Oxford in 1892, was a worthy successor to Mr Kent. The three Oxford crews stroked by him won with comparative ease, a result of which the credit in a very large share must go to Mr Pitman, who proved his judgment and coolness, not only in the races, but during practice against scratch Eights. Mr H. G. Gold's remarkable victories are too recent to require any comment beyond the statement that they stamp him as one of the company of really great strokes.

Of non-university strokes, the best I have seen have been Mr J. Hastie, of the Thames RC; Mr F. L. Playford, of the London RC; Mr J. A. Drake-Smith, of the Thames RC; and Mr G. B. James, of the London RC. The three last of these possessed, in addition to considerable natural strength and endurance, a rhythmical ease and finished elegance which made their rowing a pleasure to the eye, and rendered it easy for a crew to shake together behind them. Mr Hastie had enormous power and perfect judgment, and no man ever knew better exactly how and when to crack up an opposing crew.

NO. 7

This position is every whit as important as that of stroke. Indeed, I have known many crews that were made by a good

No. 7, in spite of an inferior or an inexperienced stroke. Of the converse I cannot at this moment remember any instances. No. 7 is the keystone of the crew. If he fits perfectly into his place, the whole fabric remains firm; if he fits badly, it will crumble to pieces at the first shock.

It is the duty of No. 7 to weld the two sides of the crew into harmony, to transmit to the rest of the crew the initiative of the stroke-oar, to be ever on the watch to make stroke's task an easy one by following him implicitly and immediately. But, more than this, a good No. 7 can control and manage an inexperienced stroke, can check him when he attempts to hurry unduly, can inspirit him and renew his energies when he shows signs of flagging. The style and elegance of a crew depend even more upon No. 7 than they do upon stroke. Therefore select for this position a man whose movements are graceful, rhythmical and easy, who can show style in his own rowing, and thus instil it into the rest of the crew. It is important for No. 7 that he too should be able to economize his power in a race. I do not mean that he is to be a 'sugarer' (a word we use to indicate a man who may show style, but who never works honestly), but he must row with judgment. I have seen many very big men row well at No. 7, but I should always prefer a man of the stamp of the late Mr H. E. Rhodes, the late Mr T. C. Edwards-Moss, Mr R. P. P. Rowe, and Mr W. E. Crum. These were all born No. 7's, though the reputation of the first was chiefly gained at stroke. Still, I consider that his best rowing was shown in 1876, when he rowed No. 7 of the Cambridge crew behind Mr C. D. Shafto. Those who can recall the marvellous flexibility and adaptable ease of Mr T. C. Edwards-Moss, and who have seen similar qualities exhibited by Mr Rowe and Mr Crum, will realize what I mean when I insist upon the importance of grace, rhythm, and elegance, in a word, of style in a No. 7. You can rarely, of course, count upon such a paragon for your No. 7, but at any rate get a man who approaches more nearly than the rest to this ideal.

NO. 6

This, again, is a very important place; for your No. 6 must back up stroke, and must, by genuine hard work, take as much as possible of the burden off stroke's shoulders. Choose for the position a man who combines great weight and power and endurance with a large share of experience, a man who can row every stroke hard, and by his swing can help to keep it long. Mr S. D. Muttlebury, in the Cambridge crews of 1886 and 1887, was such a No. 6. Such, too, was Mr W. A. L. Fletcher, in the Oxford and Leander crews of a later date, and such is the veteran Mr Guy Nickalls at the present time. It must be an inspiration to the rest of the crew to have the broad back of this iron oarsman swinging up and down with an untiring vehemence, and slogging at every stroke as if he had no thought whatever of the strokes that had to come after. But then Mr Nickalls is equally at home at No. 5 in an Eight; and as stroke-oar of a Four or pair – a position from which he invariably steers the boat – he is to my mind unapproachable. He would not himself assert that he was a model of elegance, but for power and endurance, and for the knack of infusing these qualities into the rest of the crew, no man has ever, in my experience, surpassed, and very few indeed have equalled, him.

NO. 5 AND NO. 4

These two are places which require weight and power. The details of elegance and polish are not here so important, though it is, of course, well to secure them if you can. A No. 5 who swings long and steadily is of the utmost value, and the same may be said of No. 4. For instance, no small part of the merit of the Oxford and Leander crews in which he rowed was due to Mr W. B, Stewart, their No. 5. A very tall, well-built, and extremely powerful man, he rowed, I think, with the longest swing I have ever seen. It was for this quality that we picked him out of his college crew, when he was a comparative novice, and gave him No. 5's seat in the Leander crew of 1893, and his rowing in that crew and in others subsequently proved the correctness of our judgment. The late Mr T. H. E. Stretch, too, was a remarkable No. 5, a position in which, however, he only rowed once, viz. in the Leander crew of 1896. He was then certainly, for style and power combined, the best heavyweight oar at Henley Regatta. Mr Broughton, of the Thames Rowing Club, was another fine example of what a No. 5 ought to be – a really slashing oar of wonderful power. I might use the same words to describe Mr R. S. Kindersley, of the Oxford crews of 1880, 1881, and 1882. Among good No. 4's, I should specially select Mr S. Swann, in the Cambridge crew of 1884; Mr C. B. P. Bell, of the Cambridge crews of 1888 and 1889; and Mr F. E. Robeson, of the splendid Oxford crew of 1892.

NO. 3 AND NO. 2

Of these positions little need be said. Weight here ceases to be of great importance compared with briskness and liveliness of movement. Yet instances are not wanting of genuine heavy weights who rowed at No. 3 in fast crews. Mr E. F. Henley, in the Oxford crew of 1866, rowed at 12 stone 13 lbs; Mr P. W. Taylor, in the Oxford crew of 1885, and Mr W. B. Stewart, in the Oxford crew of 1894, were placed at No. 3 in spite of their weighing well over 13 stone; and Mr Vivian Nickalls, in the Leander crew of 1891, was little short of this weight. But where these cases have occurred, they were generally due to the fact that the authorities had at their disposal a great number of really good heavy-weights, and, rather than lose one of them, they placed him at No. 3.

BOW

Bow should be light, alert, compact, springy and cat-like, and a good waterman. Such discomforts as may exist in a boat seem to concentrate themselves at bow's seat. He has less room than any other man in the boat, and any unsteadiness affects him more. I can recall a long list of good bows, but none better than Mr W. A. Ellison of Oxford, Mr R. G. Gridley of Cambridge, Mr C. W. Hughes of the Thames RC, Mr W. F. C. Holland and the late Mr H. B. Cotton of Oxford, and Mr C. W. N. Graham of Leander fame. The last two rarely rowed as much as ten stone, but their work was remarkable. In their respective college crews, they proved that they could row at stroke just as well as at the other end of the boat.

Finally, a captain of a crew must remember, if with these great examples before his eyes he feels inclined, as he runs over his list of available oars, to despair of getting together a good crew, that wonderful results have been achieved by college captains who had to draw their men from a comparatively narrow field, and were often forced by the exigencies of the case to fill places in their boats with men who were far removed from ideal perfection.

Combined Oarsmanship in Eights (continued)

From the hints given in the preceding chapter it will have been gathered that good oarsmen are of all sizes and weights. But it must not be forgotten that no small part of the motive power of a crew comes from heavy men. By weight I do not, of course, mean that which results from mere adipose deposit; but weight, as it is usually found among young men that depends on the size of the frame and the limbs, and on their due covering of muscle and sinew. I cannot, therefore, too strongly advise a captain or a coach to spare no labour and no patience in endeavouring to teach big men how to row. There will be disappointments. Everyone who has experience of rowing must remember at least one massive and magnificent giant who failed to learn, in spite of infinite pains on his own part and on the part of those who had to teach him. Out of a boat he may have looked the very model of what a heavyweight oarsman should be – erect, strong, well-proportioned, supple, and active. But put him in a boat, and at once he suffered a river change. His muscles turned into pulp, his chest became hollow, his arms and legs were mere nerveless attachments, and his whole body assumed the shapelessness of a sack of potatoes. In the end, after many days, the hopeless effort had to be sadly abandoned, and the would-be oarsman returned to the rough untutored struggles of the football field, or the intoxicating delights of lawn tennis and golf. But, on the other hand, there are innumerable instances to prove that a big man who has never touched an oar before he came to Oxford or Cambridge, or joined one of the Metropolitan clubs, may, by care and perseverance, be turned into the pride and mainstay of his crew. Therefore, I say, persist with big and heavy men, in spite of occasional discouragements; for there is more advantage to a crew in one rough thirteen-stoner who really works and swings than in two lightweights polished *ad unguem*.

In the shapes of oarsmen, again, every kind of variety may be found, not merely in minor details, but in the whole physical characteristics of their bodies. Bob Coombes, the professional champion of 1846, 1847, and 1851, has recorded his opinion that the best physical type of oarsman is the man who is, among other things, deep-chested and straight and full in the flanks; who, in other words, has no waist to speak of. To this type Mr S. D. Muttlebury and Mr Guy Nickalls conform, and there can be no doubt that it is the best. But I have known oarsmen who varied from it in every detail, and yet did magnificent work in a crew. I have already mentioned Mr C. W. Kent, and I may add another example in Mr H. Willis, of the Leander Club, a very finished and valuable oar, who has given his proofs not only in an Eight, but also as No. 3 of the winning Stewards' Four at Henley Regatta this year. Mr Willis is tall and loose jointed. He is not furnished with any great quantity of muscle, and his modesty will not resent my adding that, though he has a well-framed chest, he also possesses a very distinct waist. I might multiply such instances; but they may all be summed up in the statement that a really good oarsman is never of a bad shape – for rowing. The ultimate test is to be found not in the examination of his muscle or the measurement of his frame, but in the careful and patient observation of his work while he is actually engaged in rowing. A mere weed, of course, cannot row to advantage; but I have seen more than one instance of so-called weeds who eventually developed under the influence of the exercise into solid and capable oars. And, as a rule, there is more promise in the comparative weakling than in the gymnast whose tight binding of muscles impedes the freedom and alertness of his limbs.

We may now consider how the practice of an ordinary eight-oared crew should be conducted. There is a certain amount of difference of opinion as to how long a crew should remain in their tub – that is, in their clinker-built boat – before taking to the racing ship. Most college captains, I think, keep their men in the heavy boat too long. Four or five days are, I think, an amply sufficient period. Experienced oars are none the better for rowing in a heavy boat, and novices who have much to learn in watermanship, and want a long period for the learning, can be taught the requisite lessons only in a light ship. The difficulties of sitting such a ship are, as a rule, much exaggerated; and the young oar who watches the scratch crews rowing against a university crew, or sees a Leander Eight setting out for the first time, is apt to be surprised when he notes how eight men, who have never rowed together before, can move along with uniformity and steadiness. There are, no doubt, difficulties of balance and quickness in light ship rowing; but the sooner these are faced the better for all concerned. I am assuming, of course, that the novice has been already drilled in the manner described in previous chapters.

As to the total length of the period of practice from the start to the day of the race, that must, and does, vary according to circumstances. A university crew practising for a long race will be at work generally from about the middle of January until towards the end of March, some ten weeks in all. Cambridge college crews have six weeks, Oxford college crews only about four, for the college races. A London, Thames, or Kingston crew can command at least seven weeks for the practice of its Henley crew. On the other hand, no winning Leander crew that I have known has ever practised for more than three weeks as a combination; though individual members of it, who had not been at work since the previous year, may have been taking rowing exercise on their own account for some little time before the eight got to work. As a typical example, I may take the remarkable Leander crew of 1896. Five members of this crew – Mr Guy Nickalls, Mr J. A. Ford, Mr C. W. N. Graham, Mr T. H. E. Stretch, and Mr H. Willis – had had no rowing exercise for a year; one, Mr W. F. C. Holland, had not worked, except for a casual regatta in Portugal, since the final of the Grand Challenge Cup in 1893; the other two, Mr H. Gold and Mr R. Carr, had been in regular practice at Oxford or at Putney since the previous October. Two weeks before practice in the Eight began, Messrs Holland, Ford, Stretch, and Graham began work in a Four, with Mr Graham, the eventual bow of the Eight, at stroke. Mr Willis had half this period of preliminary practice in a pair. Mr Nickalls had for some weeks been working at Putney in a Four and a pair. Just three clear weeks before the first day of Henley Regatta the Eight was launched; but it was not until three days after this that Mr Nickalls was able to come into the boat, and the crew for the first time rowed in its final order, the advent of Mr Nickalls resulting in four changes in its arrangement. And yet this crew defeated Yale University, who had been practising for months, and other crews, composed of good material, that had been together for six or seven weeks. I have in my mind, too, another crew, a combination of three Oxonians, two Cantabs, two Etonians, and one Radleian, who, on one week's practice, managed to beat over a one-mile course the Eights of the London and Thames clubs, in spite of their ten or eleven weeks of practice.

I do not wish to have it inferred from the foregoing facts that in my opinion those crews are likely to turn out best which practise together for a very short time. Still, the qualities of skill, keenness of enthusiasm, strength, condition, and racing ability, are factors in success even more important than length of practice. It ought, of course, to be true that if you could get two crews equally matched as regards these qualities that which had had the longer period of practice should win because of its greater uniformity. Moreover, in most cases extra length of practice up to a certain point ought to imply superiority of condition. Beyond that point a crew, though it maintains its outward uniformity and style, will fall off in pace, because overwork will have dulled the edge of its energies, and robbed it of the brisk animation that marks the rowing of men trained to the very needlepoint of perfect condition. And on the whole, taking condition and the risks of staleness into account, I should prefer to take my chances for an ordinary race with a crew that had practised from four to five weeks, rather than with one that had been at it for ten or eleven. I leave out of account the Oxford and Cambridge boat race, both because of the length of the course over which it is rowed, and on account of the frequent changes to which the authorities generally find themselves compelled to resort. And even for this race, if a president could at the outset be absolutely certain as to the general composition of the crew, he would find, I think, that a period of seven weeks at the outside would be fully sufficient for him and his men. The whole matter amounts to this, that a captain or a coach must consider carefully all the circumstances of his case – the skill, the condition, the experience and the strength of his men, and the distance over which they have to race, and must decide on the period of practice accordingly. I cannot on paper lay down any fixed general rule for his guidance, but can only bring before him a few detached considerations which may be useful to him as food for reflection. For my own part, I may add that I have never found the least difficulty, even after a year's rest from rowing, in getting into very good racing condition on three or four weeks of work.

HOW TO ARRANGE THE DAILY WORK OF AN EIGHT

Let the real hard work be done in the earlier stages of practice. You thus accustom your men to one another, and you grind them into a uniformity which makes all their subsequent work easier. This plan has been very successfully followed by Oxford crews. Before they get to Putney they will have rowed over the long course of four miles some ten times. As a result, the men are hard and row well together; and during their stay at Putney it is found possible to ease them in their work, so as to bring them fresh and vigorous to the post on the day of the race. Supposing you have five weeks for practice, you ought, I think, during the first fortnight to row your crew over the racing course at least four times. During the next ten days one full course will be sufficient. The work of the last ten days must vary according to the condition of the men, but two half courses and one full course at a racing stroke will probably be found sufficient. Save for the rare case of an exceptionally long row, a practice of about an hour and a half every day is enough. At Henley all crews practise twice a day, but I do not think they spend more than two hours, if so much, on the water every day.

RATE OF STROKE

The practice rate for paddling ought not in the early stages to be less than twenty-eight to the minute, which you may raise two points when rowing hard. Later on, when your men are doing their rowing work at thirty-six or more, and when they are, or ought to be, well together, you may drop the rate of paddling to twenty-six or twenty-five, in order to give them periods of rest, and to instil into them that steadiness of swing which they are apt to neglect when engaged in the effort of working up the stroke to racing pace. For a course of a mile to a mile and a half, a crew should be able to start at forty, continue at thirty-eight, and, if necessary, finish at forty in the race. Even for the Putney to Mortlake course a crew ought to be able to command forty at a pinch. As a rule, however, over a four-mile course a crew will go quite fast enough if it starts for not more than a minute at thirty-seven to thirty-eight, and continues, in the absence of a head-wind at an average of thirty-five. At Henley most crews will start off at forty-one to forty-two for the first minute, and continue at thirty-nine. Anything higher than this is dangerous, though on a course of two-thirds of a mile I have known a Four to row forty-six in the first minute with advantage.

These instructions are intended to apply to light racing ships. For the clinker-built fixed-seat boats that are used at Oxford and Cambridge for the Torpids and Lent races, a racing rate of thirty-seven ought to be high enough, seeing that the crews are mainly composed of young oars. The second division crews of the Cambridge 'May' races row with slides, but in heavy, clinker-built boats. The advantages of this arrangement are not obvious. Still, these crews ought to be able to race at thirty-six to thirty-seven. As a rule, however, when I have seen them practising a minute's spurt, nearly all of them seem to have imagined that thirty-two strokes were amply sufficient for racing purposes.

PADDLING

Paddling should be to rowing what an easy trot is to racing speed on the cinder-path. A crew when paddling is not intended to exert itself unduly, but to move at a comfortable pace which excludes any sense of fatigue, and enables the men to give their best attention to perfecting themselves in style, and to harmonizing their individual movements with those of the rest. In paddling men do not slash at the beginning so hard, nor do they grind the rest of the stroke through with the same power as when rowing. Less violent energy is put into the work, and the stroke consequently does not come through so fast. The rate of paddling must therefore be slower than that of rowing, since each stroke takes a longer time for its completion. As a rule, too, the blade is in paddling not quite so deeply covered, and cannot make the same rushing swirl under water. During the earlier stages of practice paddling is merely easier rowing; it is not so sharply distinguished from hard rowing as it becomes later on. At the outset it is necessary to make your crew both paddle and row with a full swing, in order to get length ineradicably fixed in their style. But later on a coach may tell his men, when he asks them to paddle, not only to use the easier movements prescribed above, but also to rest themselves additionally by using a somewhat shortened swing. Then, when they are to row, he must call on them to swing forward and reach out longer; to swing back harder and longer, with a more vigorous beginning; and to put more force into their leg drive. A very useful plan, especially for the purpose of getting a crew finally together, is to make them do long stretches of paddling varied here and there by about a dozen or twenty strokes of rowing, care being taken, however, not to allow the paddling to get dead and dull, and a special point being made of getting the rowing not only hard, but very long.

Paddling is a difficult art to learn, and only the very best crews paddle really well with balance, rhythm, and ease. Many a time I have seen a good crew and an inferior one paddling along the course together, and almost invariably the good crew, which had mastered the trick of paddling at a slow stroke and with perfect ease, was distanced. Yet a moment afterwards, when they ranged up alongside, and started together for a two minutes' burst of rowing, the good crew would leave its opponents as though they were standing still.

HOW TO WORK THE STROKE UP TO RACING PACE

There comes a time in the history of every crew when, having been plodding along comfortably at thirty-four, they suddenly realize that the race is barely a week off, that if they are to have any chance of success they must raise the stroke, and that they don't know how on earth it is to be done, seeing that they have usually felt pretty well cleaned out after rowing even a half course at their present rate. However, they generally do manage *tant bien que mal* to get it done, and find in the end that thirty-eight is not really much more difficult for men in good training than thirty-four.

The best plan, I think, is to devote the greater part of an afternoon's practice to short rows of half a minute and a minute at, say, thirty-seven, and to wind up with three minutes of this. On that day there will probably be at first a terrible amount of rushing and splashing. On the following day you will find that things have settled down, and you will be able to row for five minutes at the faster rate. On the third day practise short pieces again at thirty-eight, thirty-nine, forty; and on the fourth day row your full course at as fast a rate as you can command. A coach should impress upon his crew that a fast stroke is to be secured not by rushing forward with the bodies, but by rattling away the hands quicker and by increasing the force employed in forcing the oar through the water. The pace of the bodies on the forward swing, though, of course, it does increase, should feel as if it were slower. Relatively to the rate of stroke used, it is, in fact, slower at a fast than at a slow stroke. The best stroke oars have been men who fully realized this, and who, either in breaking from a paddle into a row, or in spurting during a hard piece of rowing, gave their crew a delightful sense of steadiness and balance, which enabled them to put their utmost energies into every stroke.

PRACTICE IN STARTING

During the week preceding the race a coach should devote a great part of his attention to the task of getting his crew quick off the mark. If a crew starts in a brisk and lively manner, and gets pace on its boat immediately, it is far more likely to continue well, so long as its strength and condition last, than a crew that ponderously drags its boat off, with the notion that it can put pace on later. At the end of half a minute the lively crew would be well ahead – no small moral advantage where two crews are evenly matched. The best position for the first stroke is a little more than half forward with the body and three parts forward with the slide. The mind, as well as the muscles, must be intent on the effort. At the word 'Go' at once cover the blade deeply, spring the body on to the work, use the arms vigorously on this occasion only, and, above all, drive, drive, drive with the legs, wrenching the stroke fully home with outside hand. Then make a special point of rattling hands out like lightning, and get hold of the second stroke when the hands are over the stretcher. Again a lightning rattle, followed by a longer swing. The fourth stroke should be a full one. During the first two strokes the crew should watch stroke's blade, and take their time from that.

THE NECESSITY OF BEING EXHAUSTED

I hold it to be absolutely necessary that during practice men should learn thoroughly to row themselves out. If they do not, they need never expect to become properly fit for the hard strain involved in a race. If men will only consent to put their best and hardest work into a practice course, so that they may feel at the end of it that they have neither wind nor strength left, I will guarantee that all the subsequent work will become infinitely easier for them, and the race itself will be a pleasure instead of a pain. I hate to see a crew finish a practice row, no matter how short it may be, in perfectly fresh trim. That is a sign that they must have shirked their work. Yet I have often read in newspaper reports of the practice of crews some statement like the following: – 'The boat travelled well all through, and the time accomplished was fast; but when it was over most of the men were much distressed' – as if this were a reproach instead of a compliment. Such 'distress' is one of the necessary stages through which crews must pass on their way to good physical condition and perfect racing power. If a crew never tires itself in practice, it will never row fast in a race.

HOW TO JUDGE A MAN'S WORK IN A BOAT

This can only be done properly by watching both the movements of the body and the action of the blade in the water. It may be assumed that if the blade strikes the water fairly at the full reach, is covered at once, produces a deep boiling swirl under the water, and remains covered to the end of the stroke, the oarsman who wields it must be working, in spite of many possible faults of form. Again, if the body moves well, and with a vigorous briskness through the stroke, it may be found that the swirl of the blade through the water does not show properly, because the blade is put in too deep. This, of course, is a fault, for the oarsman is giving himself too much work, and the effect on the propulsion of the boat is smaller; but, at any rate, there is honesty of intention. On the other hand, a man may make a great show of form with his body, and a great splash in the water, by merely covering half his blade through the stroke, or by missing his beginning and rowing light at the finish; or he may seem to be swinging his body on to his work, and yet by some subtly contrived disconnection between body and arms and legs, produce no effect on the water. For all this a coach must be on the lookout. If he has once done hard rowing himself, and watched it in others, he will never mistake the sham article (the 'sugarer') for the genuine, though possibly clumsy, worker.

THE VALUE OF TUB PAIR PRACTICE

Practice in the tub pair is one of the greatest possible aids towards the consolidation of an eight-oared crew. A coach or captain should never omit during the early stages of work to take out his men two by two in a tub. Sitting at ease in the stern, he can lecture them to his heart's content, and can devote himself with far better effect than when his crew are in the Eight to eradicating individual faults and drilling the men into one uniform style. During the latter part of training, however, the tub pair is, with rare exceptions, an unnecessary burden. The crew then require all their energies for the work of the Eight, in which they ought to be learning the last important lessons of watermanship and uniformity every day. To drag them into tub pairs at such a time can only weary them.

Of Ailments – Of Training and Diet – Of Staleness – Of Discipline – Of Coaching

AILMENTS

I may preface what I have to say about ailments by stating, as emphatically as it can be stated, that every man who proposes to take part in a race ought, before he begins practice, to be thoroughly overhauled by a medical man. I do not believe that any man whose heart and lungs and general constitution are sound can be injured by rowing. On the contrary, I have seen scores and scores of instances in which sound but imperfectly developed youngsters were formed and solidified and made into robust men by the exercise. But if a doctor reports of an apparently powerful man that his heart is weak and his circulation defective, or that the state of his lungs is unsatisfactory, no power on earth would induce me to include him in my crew. Race rowing is one of the severest strains to which a man can submit himself, and only a perfectly sound man can go through it without taking harm.

Coaches are sometimes ridiculed for the excessive care they take of their men; and there are not wanting those who draw the inference that rowing men are peculiarly liable to illness, and suffer, when attacked by it, more than others. Nothing can be further from the truth. If we are anxious, it is because we know that for the special strain involved in racing a man must be in especially good condition, and we desire, above all things, to avoid anything that may keep him back in his training and his work. Moreover, even a slight illness may entail temporary retirement from the crew, and thus necessitate changes in its order which will prevent the men from getting together.

In rowing hard a man should keep a good colour. If you see him turning green and yellow, you may be sure that something is wrong with him, and you must pack him off to the doctor at once. It may turn out that his digestion is in fault, and that a careful attention to diet is all that is necessary to cure him. I have seen only two men actually faint during a race. One of them was a distinguished Oxford Blue, who collapsed during a heat of the Grand Challenge Cup at Henley; the other was a college oar rowing in the Cambridge Fours. With regard to him, we discovered afterwards that he had overtaxed his strength by working in the Cambridge engineering workshop for about six hours every day. Both these cases took place a good many years ago, and in neither has any permanent injury resulted. I have, of course, seen hundreds of men absolutely rowed out at the end of a race; but, with hardly an exception, they were perfectly fit a few minutes afterwards and, possibly, in the course of a few hours they might be seen rowing in another severe race with unimpaired strength and vitality.

With regard to ailments generally, I cannot do better than quote Mr Woodgate in the Badminton book:

> A crew should be under strict orders to report all ailments, if only a blister, instantly to the coach. It is better to leave no discretion in this matter to the oarsman, even at the risk of troubling the mentor with trifles. If a man is once allowed to decide for himself whether he will report some petty and incipient ailment, he is likely to hush it up, lest it should militate against his coach's selection of him. The effect of this is that mischief which might otherwise have been checked in the bud, is allowed to assume dangerous proportions for want of a stitch in time. An oarsman should be impressed that nothing is more likely to militate against his dream of being selected than disobedience to this or any other standing order. The smallest pimple should be shown forthwith to the coach

– verily the coach is not only διος, but πολυτλαςπολυτλας – 'the slightest hoarseness or tendency to snuffle reported, any tenderness of joint or sinew instantly made known.'

To these golden words I would merely add that in all more serious cases, such as boils, colds, coughs, severe diarrhoea, or strains, it is best for the coach not to attempt any amateur doctoring, but to send his oarsman at once to a qualified doctor. In nearly every large rowing club, and at the universities, there are to be found doctors who have either rowed themselves, or have had long experience of treating the ailments of rowing men; and it is far better to take their advice, which, as a rule, does not incline to mollycoddling, than to run the risk of losing a valuable oar out of the crew through one's own quackery.

BLISTERS

Blisters are a common accompaniment of the early days of practice. They are ordinarily innocuous enough if well treated; but a neglected blister may result in a raw hand, and lead to blood-poisoning. The best plan is to prick a blister at its side with a clean needle before going to bed, and on the following day or two to row with a glove and a pad of cotton wool over the blister. The skin very soon hardens into a callosity.

BOILS

These are a sure sign that the blood is in a bad condition, due probably to overeating. They afflict novices much more often than old oars, who have learnt by experience to diet themselves. A mild dose of Eno's Fruit Salt before breakfast may be recommended. The quantity of beef and mutton eaten must be largely reduced. Fish and the dark meat of poultry should be the staple articles of diet, and not too much of those. Nor must the mistake be made of making up for the decrease of meat by overloading the stomach with immense masses of vegetables, though in moderation vegetables are excellent. Having thus done his best for the patient's inside, the coach must send him to a doctor to have the boil treated externally.

DIARRHOEA

Cut off fruits of all kinds; reduce meat; give an extra glass of port, and if the complaint continues, send the afflicted to a doctor.

STRAINS

Ordinary muscular strains generally yield to a good rubbing with an embrocation. For wrist strains a leather band may be recommended. Abdominal strains must be seen to by a doctor.

COLDS

The best remedy for a severe cold is to give your man at least one day's complete rest, and make him keep his room. Indeed, with most ailments a day's rest will work wonders; and it is far better for a coach to make up his reluctant mind to grant it, than to run the risk of losing a valuable man altogether by keeping him chained to his oar when he is unfit to work. However, no man who takes proper care of himself, and always makes a point of wrapping up when his crew easies, ought to catch a cold.

TRAINING AND DIET

The rules of training and diet should be the rules of common sense, applied to cases in which the body has to prepare itself, by severe work and perfectly simple, healthy living, for an exceptional effort or series of efforts. Rules there must be, if only on account of the advantage that comes of being able to make exceptions to them. But the chief points must be regularity and simplicity – a regularity, that is, which shall not entail an unvarying and wearisome monotony, and simplicity which shall not exclude occasional little luxuries that act as a stimulus to a man's jaded energies.

I shall give here two tables showing the hours and the dietary of an Oxford crew training during a little more than five weeks for the race against Cambridge, and of a Leander crew training for nearly three weeks for the Grand Challenge race at Henley Regatta.

I. Oxford Crew.
7.00 a.m. – Out of bed and, without bathing or washing, dress immediately in flannels. A cup of milk and a biscuit.
7.15 a.m. – Out of the house. A brisk walk with one sharp run of 150 yards.
7.50 a.m. – Back to the house. Bath, etc.

8.30 a.m. Breakfast. – Fish, plainly cooked, without sauce. Soles, whiting, and smelts are best. Salmon is not allowed. Cutlets or beefsteaks, or grilled chicken. Eggs, boiled, or poached, or fried, sometimes scrambled. Mustard and cress, or water-cress. Toast. Limited amount of butter. Marmalade is allowed only during the last fortnight of training. Not more than a cup and a half of tea.

11.00 a.m. – At Putney, when the state of the tide permits it, exercise in the boat. It should be noted that the tide sometimes makes it necessary for the crew to do its rowing in the morning, sometimes in the afternoon. Occasionally work can be done both in the morning and afternoon.

1.00 p.m. Lunch. – Cold meat. Tomatoes plainly made into a salad with oil and vinegar. Toast. Small quantity of butter. Oatmeal biscuits. One glass of draught beer, or claret and water.

3.00 p.m. or 4.00 p.m. – (according to tide). Work in the boat.

6.30 p.m. Dinner. – Fish, as at breakfast. An entrée of pigeons, or sweetbread, or spinach and poached eggs. Roast joint (not pork or veal), or else chicken, with potatoes, mashed or boiled, and boiled vegetables. Stewed fruit with rice puddings. Sometimes jelly. Two glasses of draught beer, or claret and water. For dessert, figs, prunes, oranges, dry biscuits, and one glass of port wine.

9.50 p.m. – A glass of lemon and water, or a cup of water-gruel.

10.00 p.m. – Bed.

(Note. – Once or twice during training there is a 'champagne night,' when champagne is substituted for beer or claret and water; but this only occurs when the crew have been doing very hard work, or when they show evident signs of being over-fatigued, and require a fillip.)

II. Leander Training at Henley.

7.00 a.m. to 8.30 a.m. – Same as in Oxford Crew.

8.30 a.m. Breakfast. – Same as in Oxford Crew, save for the frequent absence of meat. Marmalade allowed. Strawberries or peaches without sugar; no cream.

10.30 a.m. or 11.00 a.m., or 12 p.m. – Out on the water.

1.30 p.m. Lunch. – Same as in Oxford Crew.

4.45 p.m. – Cup of tea with a slice of bread and butter, or a biscuit.

5.30 p.m. or 6.00 p.m. – Out on the water.

7.30 p.m. or 8.00 p.m. Dinner. – Same as in Oxford Crew.

9.50 p.m. – Same as in Oxford Crew.

10.15 p.m. – Bed.

(NB. With most Leander crews, which are composed of experienced oarsmen, it has been found possible to abolish restrictions on the amount of liquor, and to allow the men to take what they want to satisfy their thirst, which at Henley time is naturally more severe than it is in the early spring at Putney. With a college crew of younger and less experienced oars such liberty of action is not to be recommended; but a trainer ought, during hot weather, to tell his men that if they really want an extra half-glass or so, they are not to hesitate to ask for it. Men in training will, however, generally find that if they exercise a little self-control during the first few days of training, when the restriction on their drink seems especially painful, their desire for drink will gradually diminish, until at last they are quite content with their limited allowance. If, on the contrary, they perpetually indulge themselves, they will always be wanting more. On this point I may cite the authority of the following remarks extracted from a recent article in the British Medical Journal: –

Among the various discomforts entailed upon us by the hot weather is thirst, which leads to many accidents. First and most especially is the danger arising from the ingestion of ices and cold drinks, which so many people fly to directly they feel hot. Difficult as it may be to explain in precise physiological terms the evil consequences which so often follow the sudden application of cold to the mucous membrane of the stomach when the body is over-heated, there is no doubt about the fact, and people would do well to remember the risk they run when they follow their instinct, and endeavour to assuage their thirst by huge draughts of cold fluids. There can be but little doubt that the profuse perspiration which is the cause of so many dangers is greatly aggravated by drinking, and especially by drinking alcoholic fluids. No one can watch a tennis match without noticing how the men perspire, while the girls hardly turn a hair. Some, perhaps, will say that the girls play the feebler game; but, game or no game, they exert themselves. The same also may be seen at any dance. The secret is that the men follow their instinct and slake their thirst, while the girls simply bear it. It should be remembered that thirst is the result of want of fluid in the blood, not want of fluid in the stomach, and that a pint or more may be drunk before a single ounce is absorbed. Any attempt, then, to assuage thirst by rapid drinking must of necessity lead to far more being taken than is wanted, the moral of which is that if we must drink, at least let us drink slowly.

Besides asking his men to drink slowly, a coach will do well to see that they take no drink at all before they have eaten a certain amount of food. Between meals, except as set out in the tables given above, no drink of any kind should be allowed.

Over-eating, too, is a very common danger, especially in the case of youngsters, and a coach must warn his crew severely against it.

A captain ought to be especially strict in insisting on getting his men out of their beds at a fixed time, and in seeing that they do not stay up too late at night. Absolute punctuality all round ought to be rigidly enforced. If, however, anybody should resent the severities entailed by this dietary, and pine for freedom, he may be recommended to try what I may call the Ouida system. It is fully set out in 'Under Two Flags,' from which, in a spirit of humble admiration, I venture to give an extract:—

Beauty don't believe in training. No more do I. Never would train for anything,' said the Seraph, now pulling the long blonde moustaches that were not altogether in character with his seraphic cognomen. 'If a man can ride, let him. If he's born to the pig-skin he'll be in at the distance safe enough, whether he smoke or don't smoke, drink or don't drink. As for training on raw chops, giving up wine, living like the very deuce, and all as if you were in a monastery, and changing yourself into a mere bag of bones – it's utter bosh. You might as well be in purgatory; besides, it's no more credit to win then than if you were a professional.

'But you must have trained at Christ Church, Rock, for the Eight?' asked another Guardsman, Sir Vere Bellingham – 'Severe,' as he was christened, chiefly because he was the easiest-going giant in existence.

'Did I! Men came to me; wanted me to join the Eight. Coxswain came, awful strict little fellow, docked his men of all their fun—took plenty himself, though! Coxswain said I must begin to train, do as all his crew did. I threw up my sleeve and showed him my arm;' and the Seraph stretched out an arm magnificent enough for a statue of Milo. 'I said, There, sir, I'll help you thrash Cambridge, if you like, but train I won't for you or for all the university. I've been captain of the Eton Eight; but I didn't keep my crew on tea and toast. I fattened 'em regularly three times a week on venison and champagne at Christopher's. Very happy to feed yours, too, if you like – game comes down to me every Friday from the Duke's moors; they look uncommonly as if they wanted it! You should have seen his face! Fatten the Eight! He didn't let me do that, of course; but he was very glad of my oar in his rowlocks, and I helped him beat Cambridge without training an hour myself, except so far as rowing hard went.'

And the Marquis of Rockingham, made thirsty by the recollection, dipped his fair moustaches into a foaming seltzer.

'Quite right, Seraph!' said Cecil. 'When a man comes up to the weights, looking like a homonunculus after he's been getting every atom of flesh off him like a jockey, he ought to be struck out for the stakes, to my mind.'

The obvious inference from this is that if we want to avoid looking like 'homonunculi' we must acquire dukes as fathers, and get fattened on venison and champagne.

SMOKING

There are no smokes in training.

STALENESS

In the practice of almost every crew there comes a period, generally about half way through training, when they begin to show the effects of hard work by a certain lassitude and loss of vigour. This, in fact, is not genuine staleness, but is the halfway house to perfect condition. An experienced coach can always detect the signs of it among his men. Their tempers will be short, they will begin to mope about the room, and their general manner will betray languor and listlessness, instead of that brisk cheerfulness that one has a right to expect. Their appetite will decrease, and at meals they will dally with their food instead of consuming it with a hearty zest. If a coach is blind to these signs, and pursues, in spite of them, the scheme of work and diet which he may have laid down at the first, he will probably bring to the post a crew as stale and lifeless as London shrimps. If, however, he grants certain indulgences to those who are most affected; if he lets them lie in bed of a morning, adds a basin of soup to their lunch or dinner, gives them extra liquor, or champagne in place of their ordinary liquor, and eases the work of the crew all round, he will probably find that within three days they will be perfectly brisk and fit again. I remember the case of an Oxford crew which showed the worst symptoms of staleness on a Friday. Saturday to Monday they spent in Brighton, and returned so reinvigorated, that on the following Wednesday they were able in the race to row Cambridge down at Chiswick and win by a length. For extreme cases of what I call genuine staleness, I do not think there is any remedy except complete rest for a period more or less prolonged. I have seen instances of this at Henley among university oarsmen, who had had practically no rest since the previous October.

DISCIPLINE

Not the least important point in the management of a crew lies in the preservation of strict discipline. While they are in the boat and engaged in rowing, no man, except the captain or the cox, should speak a word, unless he is appealed to by the coach. A wise captain, too, when he has a coach in whom he trusts, will content himself with saying very little indeed. To be constantly cursing his crew, or to be shouting directions to them from the boat, not only irritates the other men, but increases all the difficulties of a coach. To 'answer back' a coach is a capital offence, which ought to lead to immediate removal from the crew. I can only remember one instance of it in all my experience, and that was promptly followed by a humble apology. Silence, prompt obedience, absolute subordination of the individual self to the collective good of the crew, a quick and hearty willingness in endeavouring to carry out orders or instructions, a cheerful temper when things are going awry, and a constant keenness whether in rowing or paddling – these are model qualities which will go far to make a man a valuable oar. Nothing has so bad an effect upon a crew as the display of moroseness or sullenness on the part of one of its members. If that member should chance to be the captain, the baneful effects are increased tenfold. There are times of inattention and slackness when a coach does well to be angry, and to bring his men sharply back to a knowledge of their duty.

THE COACH

I cannot deal with this subject at any length, for good coaching is a matter of temperament, sympathy, tact, and intelligence – qualities that cannot be taught. The man who has these necessary qualities, and adds to them a wide experience of rowing, can never go very far wrong in coaching a crew. If a man can once establish between himself and his crew that subtle bond which comes of their conviction that their welfare and success are his chiefest desire, and that everything he says is absolutely right, the rest will be comparatively easy. A few simple hints may, however, be given.

1. Never nag at your crew, or at an individual. Point out his fault; explain to him as clearly as you can how he ought to correct it, and then leave him alone for a bit. Never weary your men with an incessant stream of talk. Periods of complete silence on your part are very valuable, to you and to the crew.

2. If you see signs of improvement in a man whom you have been correcting, never fail to tell him so. A little encouragement of this kind has more effect than heavy loads of objurgation.

3. Rebuke any carelessness very sharply, but always keep strong measures, such as taking a crew back to the start, for really serious emergencies.

4. Show no partiality, and make as little difference as you can between man and man. It is useful to begin by coaching old hands with some severity. New hands are encouraged by feeling that even a Blue or a Grand Challenge winner is liable to error, and that a coach is not afraid to tackle these eminent men.

5. Make a gallant effort never to lose your temper with an individual, though loss of temper with a crew as a whole need not always be avoided. When things go wrong in a crew, impress upon each and every man that he is individually responsible for the defects. Every man is probably doing something wrong, and in any case a determined and united attempt to row better can do no harm.

6. Never tell your men that they are rowing 'well,' or 'better,' when these statements are contrary to the truth. The men in the boat can generally feel what is happening as well as you can see it from the bank or the launch, and they are apt to lose confidence in a man who talks smooth things when everything is rough.

7. Never confuse a man by telling him more than one thing at a time while he is rowing. When the crew has eased you can lecture him and them more at length.

8. Remember Dr Warre's rule, that general exhortations, such as 'Time,' 'Beginning,' 'Smite,' 'Keep it long,' and the like, are to be given at the right moment, not used as mere parrot cries.
9. Vary the tone of your voice as much as possible.
10. Vary, if possible, the expressions you use in pointing out and correcting faults.
11. Always insist on your crew putting on their wraps when they easy after rowing hard.
12. Never allow men during summer training to stand, sit, or lie about in the full blaze of the sun.
13. Teach by example as well as by precept. The coach should be able to take his seat in a gig pair, and to show his men practically the style he wishes them to row in, and how their faults may be corrected.
14. Always remember, while paying attention to the form of individuals that your main object is to secure uniformity in the crew. Never fail, therefore, to correct faults of time instantly.

Of the Race-Day – Of the Race – Of the Necessity of Having a Butt – Of Leisure Time – Of Aquatic Axioms

THE DAY OF THE RACE

On this tremendous day, towards which all their efforts for weeks past have been directed, the coach will find that all his crew are suffering from that peculiar nervousness to which rowing men have given the name of 'the needle.' It is a complaint against which no length of experience can harden a man, and the veteran of a hundred races will feel it as acutely as the boy who is engaged in his first struggle. A sort of forced cheerfulness pervades the air. Men make irrelevant remarks about their oars, their stretchers, or the notorious incapacity of their rivals, while they are reading the newspapers or discussing the politics of the day. Even a coach is seized with the universal affection, however gallantly he may strive against it, and endeavour to entertain the crew with all his best stories of triumphant victories, of defeats averted by brilliant spurts, or of the last sayings of some well-known aquatic humourist. Old oars drop in, and for a few moments divert the conversation, only to flow back with it into the one absorbing topic that occupies all men's minds. The feeling goes on increasing until at last, oh joy! the time comes for getting into the boat. With his faithful oar in his hand, and his feet fixed to the stretcher, a man regains his confidence, and when the word is given he will find that the only effect that the needle has had upon him has been to brace his energies to their highest pitch. The duty of a coach on such an occasion is clear. He must try to keep his men cheerful, and prevent them from brooding over the race that is to come. Visits from old oars should be encouraged, for it is often a relief and an amusement to a youngster to find that some solid oar of the past is even more agitated than he is himself. One thing must not be omitted, and that is the preliminary spin, which should take place about two hours before the race, and should consist of two sharp starts of ten strokes each and one hard row of a minute. This has an invaluable effect in clearing the wind. I have always felt, when I have rowed more than one race in a day, and I think my experience will be confirmed by most other oarsmen, that I have been able to row better, harder, and with less distress, in the second race than in the first. An hour and a half before the race a man will be all the better for a biscuit and a hot cup of strong meat soup, with perhaps a dash of brandy to flavour it, but this must depend upon the hour at which the race is rowed, for if you have lunched at one and have to race at half-past three you will want nothing between times to stay your stomach. The early morning sprint should be taken as usual.

Henley Regatta, 1897. (New College v. Leander. Won by New College by 2 feet.)

THE RACE

'I shall say, "Are you ready?" once; if I receive no answer, I shall say, "Go!"' It is the voice of the umpire addressing us from the steam-launch in which he will follow the race. He must be a man dead to all feeling, incapable of sympathy, for he actually turns to one of his fellow passengers and makes a jesting remark, while our hearts are palpitating and our minds are strung up to face the stern actualities of the race. The other crew look very big and strong, and fit and determined. We shall have to row our hardest, and we all know it. 'Get the top of your shorts properly tucked in,' says our captain, 'so as not to catch your thumbs; and mind, all of you, eyes in the boat, and when cox shouts for ten strokes let her have it. Come forward all.'

'Touch her gently, bow' (it is the cox who speaks, and his voice sounds thin and far away and dream-like). 'One more. That'll do. Easy, bow. Now we're straight.'

'Are you ready?' from the umpire. Great heaven! will he never say – 'Go!' he shouts. There is a swish, a leap, a strain, a rattle of oars, a sense of something moving very swiftly alongside, a turmoil of water, a confused roar from the bank: we are off!

We started splendidly. For half a minute I am a mere machine; thoughts, feelings, energies—all are concentrated into one desire to work my hardest and to keep in time. Then my mind clears, and I become conscious once more of myself and my surroundings. Have we gained? I must steal a look. By Jupiter, they're leaving us! 'Eyes in the boat, four,' screams the cox; 'you're late!' Be hanged to cox! He's got eyes like a lynx. Yes; there's no doubt of it—I can see, without looking out of the boat, out of the corner of my eye. They're gaining still. Now their stroke is level with me; now he has disappeared, and for a few strokes I am conscious of a little demon cox bobbing and screeching alongside of me. Then he, too, draws away, and their rudder is all I can see. At last that also vanishes, and a sense of desolation descends on us. Nearly two minutes must have gone; I know that by the landmarks we have passed. Surely we ought to spurt. What can stroke be up to? Is he going to let us be beaten without an effort. Ugh! What a shower-bath that was. It's six splashing, as usual. Well, if we're beaten, we must just grin and bear it. We shall have to congratulate the other ruffians. Hateful! Somebody must get beaten. But we're not beaten yet, hang it all! Three minutes. What's this? Cox is shouting. 'Now, ten hard strokes together; swing out, and use your legs!' He counts them out for us at the top of his voice.

Grand! We're simply flying. That's something like it. And I'm
not a bit done yet. We're none of us done. The boat's going like
smoke. 'Nine!' yells the cox. 'Ten! Now, don't slack off, but keep
her going. You're gaining, you're gaining! On to it, all of you.'
He is purple in the face, and foaming at the mouth. Glorious!
Their rudder comes back to me; I see their cox. We are catching
them. Now for it! A few strokes more and the boats are running
dead level, and so they continue for half a minute. Stroke has
now, however, taken the measure of his foes. We are steadying
down and swinging longer, and I am conscious that the other
crew are rowing a faster stroke. It is now our turn to leave them.
Foot by foot we creep past them; their bows come level with me,
and then slowly recede. I can see the back of their bowman. His
zephyr has come out from his shorts; the back of his neck is very
pale. There can't be more than two minutes left now, and I'm
still fit, and my wind is all right. We are winning; I'm sure of it.
No; they're spurting again, and, by Jove! They're gaining! Spurt,
stroke, spurt! We mustn't get beaten on the post. But stroke,
that wary old warrior, knows what he is about. Unmistakable
signs prove to him that this effort is the last desperate rally of
his enemies. He sees their boat lurch; their time is becoming
erratic; two of them are rolling about in evident distress. His
own crew he has well in hand; we are rowing as one man,
and he feels that he has only to give a sign, and our restrained
eagerness will blaze forth and carry us gloriously past the post.
Let us wait, he seems to say, a very few seconds more, until the
opposing spurt fades out to its inevitable end; so he rows on
imperturbably. But isn't he running it too fine? Not he. He gives
a quick word to cox, rattles his hands away, and swings as if
he meant to strike his face against the kelson of the boat. 'Pick
her up all!' screams the cox. 'Now then!' comes in a muffled
gasp from the captain. We feel that our moment has come, and,
with a unanimous impulse, we take up the spurt and spin the
ship along. In a flash we leap ahead; we leave the other crew
as if it was standing still. We are a length ahead; now we are
clear; half a length of open water divides us from them. To all
intents and purposes the race is over. The crowd grows thicker;
the shouts from the bank become a deafening din. Enthusiasts
scream futile encouragements to pursuer and pursued, and in
another moment the flag is down, the cox cries 'Easy all!' and
with triumph in our hearts we realize that we have won. The
captain turns round to us – he is rowing No. 7 – his face glowing
with pleasure. 'Well rowed indeed, you men!' he pants. 'You all
did thundering well! And as for you, stroke,' but words fail him,

and all he can do is to clap his delighted stroke on the back. Then, having duly exchanged the customary 'Well rowed!' and its accompanying rattle of oars in rowlocks with our gallant enemy, we paddle home to the raft, where our exultant coach and our perspiring partisans receive us with hand-shakings and embraces and fervently epitomized stories of the struggle. 'I knew you had got 'em all the way!' says the coach. 'Did you hear me shout when you got to the half-way point?' 'Hear you shout?' we reply in a chorus of joyful assent. 'Of course we did. That's why we spurted.' Of course, we had heard nothing; but at this moment we almost think we did hear him plainly, and in any case we are not going to be so churlish as to detract from anybody's joy over our victory.

And so the struggle is ended, and we have won. Pleasant though it is to know that training is over, there is not one of us who does not feel a sense of sorrow as he realizes that these days of toil and hardship and self-restraint, of glorious health and vigorous effort are past. All the little worries under which we chafed, the discipline that at times was irksome, the thirst, the fatigue, the exhaustion, the recurrent disappointments – all these become part of a delightful memory. Never again, it may be, shall these eight men strike the sounding furrows together. The victory that has crowned us with honour has at the same time broken up our companionship of labour and endurance; but its splendid memory, and the friendships it knit together – these remain with us, and are a part of our lives henceforth wherever we may be.

THE NECESSITY OF HAVING A BUTT

Let me turn now to lighter matters, for there are lighter matters connected with rowing. And first let me insist on the necessity of having a butt in a crew. It appears strange at first sight that the system of training – that is to say, of diet, of early hours, of healthy exercise, and of perfect regularity in all things, which has so admirable an effect upon the condition of the body, should sometimes impair the powers of the mind, and absolutely shatter the temper. I have seen eight healthy, happy, even-tempered young men go into training together for three weeks. They were all the best of friends. Tom had known Dick at school, and both had been inseparable from Harry ever since they had gone up to the university. With these three the other five were closely linked by a common pursuit and by common interests. Each one of them was a man of whom his friends could say, he was the easiest man to get on with you could possibly meet. Yet mark what happened. At the end of three weeks every man in that crew was the proud possessor of seven detested foes. They ate their food in morose silence; they took no delight in the labour of the oar, and each one confided to his outside friends his lamentable opinions about the seven other members of the crew. Even now, though years have passed away, no one who rowed in that crew can look back without horror on those three terrible weeks. Why was this so? The simple answer is this, that the crew in question did not number among its members a butt. I doubt if the importance of a butt in modern boat racing has been properly recognized. Speaking from an experience of many years, I should affirm unhesitatingly, if I did not remember what I have written in previous chapters, that in an ordinary crew, composed, as ordinary crews are, of men and not of angels, the position of butt is a far more important and responsible one than that of stroke or No. 7. If you can find a good, stout, willing butt – a butt who lends himself to nicknames, and has a temper as even as a billiard-table and as long as a tailor's bill – secure him at once and make him the nucleus of your crew. There may be difficulties, of course, if he should happen to be a heavy weight without a notion of oarsmanship, but these defects can easily be mitigated by good coaching, and in any case they cannot be allowed to count against the supreme merit of keeping the rest of the crew in good temper. Salient characteristics are apt to be a rock of offence to a training crew. To be a silent thinker does not give rise to happiness in the seven who watch you think. It is an even deadlier thing to be an eloquent gabbler or a dreary drawler. There is nothing an ordinary rowing man detests so much as windy eloquence, unless it be perhaps the miserable indolence which is known as slackness. The butt must therefore be neither silent, nor slack, nor a drawler. Nature will probably have saved him from being a thinker or an orator. He must be simply good-natured without affectation, and ready to allow tempers made stormy by rowing and training to break upon his broad back without flinching. Your true butt is always spoken of as 'old' so-and-so, and, as a rule, he is a man of much sharper wits, with a far keener insight into character, than most of those who buffet or tease him. Among eminent butts may be named Mr –, but on second thoughts I refrain.

LEISURE TIME

It seems a mere platitude to say that a man who can occupy his spare moments in writing or reading is likely to be happier and more even-tempered than one who is never seen with a book or a pen in his hand. Yet it is a platitude of which not many oarsmen realize the force; and, indeed, it is not an uncommon sight to see most of the members of a crew sitting about listlessly in armchairs or talking the stale futilities of rowing shop when they might with more solid advantage be engaged, let us say, in following Mr Stanley Weyman's or Dr Conan Doyle's latest hero through the mazes of his exciting adventures. At Oxford or Cambridge, of course, a man has his lectures to attend, his fixed tale of work to get through. But at Putney or at Henley this is not so. There a man is thrown back on his own resources, a companionship which he does not always seem to find particularly cheerful or attractive. A billiard table, of course, is a valuable adjunct to training quarters, but this is scarcely ever found at Henley, and not always at Putney. Besides, most of us, after a short time, cease to take any pleasure whatever in a game in which we are not qualified to shine. The joy of reading the sporting reporter's account of your doings, and of proving conclusively that he knows nothing about rowing, lasts but a short time every morning. I may, therefore, offer the oarsman a piece of advice which is, sound, in spite of its copybook flavour, and that is, that he shall cultivate a habit of reading, and, if possible, of reading good literature. Many moralists might recommend this habit on the common ground that good literature tends to improve the tone of a man's mind; and even a coach who is not a moralist will find it useful in distracting the thoughts of his men. Besides, it is quite pleasant in after life to recognize a well-worn quotation in a newspaper article, and to remember, probably with complete inaccuracy, where it originated. A little attention to writing and spelling might also prove valuable. Oarsmen who had devoted themselves, say for ten minutes a day, to these simple tasks, would have been saved from perpetrating the following correspondence, which I quote verbatim et literatim from letters in my possession: –

Dear –
It has been reported to me that you broke training last night you were seen smoking not only a few wiffs but a whole pipe I have therefore decided to turn you out of the boat.

Yours, etc.

Answer to the above: –

> Dear –
> I am in receipt of your letter it is true that I smoked two whifs (not "wiffs" as you say) out of another man's pipe but that's all however I don't want to row in your beastly boat.
>
> > Yours, etc.

AQUATIC AXIOMS

I may add here some axioms which have been printed before, but which I may venture to repeat in a treatise on rowing. The years that have passed since they were first set down have not weakened my conviction that they are accurate. I still believe myself justified in stating –

1. That if two crews row a course within ten minutes of one another, the wind is always more violent and the stream more powerful against the crew in which you yourself happen to be rowing.
2. That it is always right to take off at least five seconds from the time shown on your stopwatch in timing your own crew, and to add them, by way of compensation, to the time shown on the same watch when timing a rival crew.
3. That your own crew is absolutely the only one which ever rows the full course right out or starts at the proper place.
4. That if your crew is impeded while rowing a course you must allow ten seconds; but if any other crew is impeded you must allow only two seconds.
5. That if you row a slow course, No. 5's stretcher gave way, or his slide came off.
6. That you could always knock a quarter of a minute off when you row a faster stroke, but that –
7. You never do, as a matter of fact, row a faster stroke.
8. That your crew always rowed a slower stroke than the rest.
9. That you are sure to do a faster time tomorrow.
10. That your private opinion is, that if everybody in the crew did as much work as you do yourself your crew would be many lengths faster, and –
11. (and last) That you always lose by the steering of your coxswain three lengths, which all other crews gain by the steering of theirs.

Four-Oars and Pair-Oars – Swivel Rowlocks

Henley Regatta. (A Heat for the Diamonds.)

A good coxswainless four-oared crew represents skill and watermanship, as distinguished from mere brute strength, in their highest development. I may lay it down as an axiom that any man who can row well in a coxswainless Four will row equally well in an eight-oared crew. The converse of this is, however, by no means true. A man may do good work in an Eight, and yet be incapable of doing himself justice in a Four, or, indeed, of helping the pace of the boat in any way. Rowing of a more refined order is requisite for a Four. Greater power of balance is needed, and a more perfect sense of that rhythm which goes far to secure uniformity in rowing. You may have in your Eight a clumsy heavyweight, who at No. 5 can use his strength to wonderful advantage, in spite of various aberrations from correct form. But if you put this man at No. 3

in a Four, the results are sure to be disastrous. An easier style of movement is required for a Four. A strenuous application of all the bodyweight at the beginning of the stroke is still, no doubt, necessary. The beginning must, of course, be gripped, and that firmly; but the best four-oared rowing I have seen always gave me the impression that a sort of 'oiling' method of progression, in which steady leg pressure plays a prominent part, was best suited to a Four which is not encumbered with the weight of a coxswain. Over and over again have Eights been defeated at Henley for the Grand Challenge Cup, and yet Fours, selected from their members, have been able to beat all comers in the Stewards'. From 1868 to 1878 the London Rowing Club won the Grand five times. In the same period of eleven years their Four was only once defeated for the Stewards', proving, if any proof were needed, that an inferior Eight (I use the term merely relatively) may contain a first-class victorious Four. On the other hand, from 1891 to 1897, a period during which Leander won the Grand five times, they were able to win the Stewards' only once, and that was this year, when their Eight was defeated. Instances of this kind might be multiplied.

But besides skill in oarsmanship, another element, which adds greatly both to the difficulties and pleasures of a Four, has to be considered. This is the necessity that one of the oarsmen should not only row, but also guide the course of the boat by steering with his foot. It is evident that watermanship of a very high order is needed for this feat. The steerer must know the course and all its points perfectly. The ordinary oar often finds it difficult to keep time when his eyes are glued on the back of the men in front of him, but the steerer in a Four has to keep time and regularity, even though he may be forced to look round in order to ascertain the true direction of his boat. An oarsman in an Eight has both his feet firmly fixed; a steerer of a Four must keep one foot constantly ready for movement. And all this he has to do without making the boat roll, or upsetting the harmony of his crew. These difficulties, no doubt, are great; but when once they have been overcome, and the crew has shaken absolutely together, there can be few pleasures in the world of exercise comparable to that of rowing in a Four.

During a long period the London Rowing Club had almost a monopoly of good Fours. Their crews showed a degree of watermanship which in those days university oarsmen despaired of attaining to. Gulston, Stout, A. de L. Long, Trower, S. Le, and B. Smith were not only names to conjure with, but showed in their rowing that perfection of apparently simple ease which lies at the root of success in four-oared rowing. Who that ever witnessed it can forget the sight, once well-known at Henley, of Mr F. S. Gulston as he rowed and steered his Four to victory? As a recent Cambridge versifier said of him –

> They can't recall, but ah, I can,
> How hard and strong you looked, sir;
> Twelve stone, and every ounce a man,
> Unbeatable, uncooked, sir.
> Our French friends, had they seen your rude
> Vast strength had cried, 'Ah quel beau
> Rameur, celui qui arque le coude'—
> That is, protrudes his elbow.

> Your ship could run like Charley's Aunt,
> And you, demure as Penley,
> Knew all the wiles that might enchant
> The river nymphs at Henley.
> No piles had yet marked out the way
> Forbidding men to try on
> The tricks that found round every bay
> The short cuts to the 'Lion.'

> Each inch of bay you knew by heart,
> You knew the slackest water;
> All foes who faced you at the start,
> You beat, and beat with slaughter.
> To 'form' a stranger, yet your style
> The kind that much endures was.
> I never saw – forgive the smile –
> A rounder back than yours was.

> But round or straight, when all dismayed
> Your rivals lagged in trouble,
> Still with a firm, unfaltering blade
> You drove the swirling bubble.
> With you to speed the hours along
> No day was ere spent dully,
> Our stalwart, cheerful, matchless, strong,
> Our undefeated Gully.

As a matter of record it may be stated that Mr. Gulston won five Grand Challenge Cup medals and ten Stewards' Cup medals, Mr A. de L. Long five Grand Challenge Cup medals and eight

Stewards' Cup medals, Mr S. Le, and B. Smith four Grand Challenge Cup medals, and seven Stewards' Cup medals. No oarsman of the present day can boast of anything like such a record in these two events.

The art of four-oared rowing, then, was brought to perfection by the crews of the London Rowing Club many years ago; but there is no danger that it will be forgotten by oarsmen of the present day. Indeed, the rowing of the Leander Four that won the Stewards' Cup this year was about as good as four-oared rowing can be. They were absolutely together, they rowed with most perfect ease, and in the race they beat record time by seven seconds, and might have beaten it by still more, had they not eased a length or two from the finish. Their weights were as follows: –

Bow – C. W. N. Graham 10 stone 2 lbs.

2 – J. A. Ford 12 stone 1 lb.

3 – H. Willis 11 stone 12 lbs.

Guy Nickalls (stroke, and steers) 12 stone 7 lbs.

From the above remarks it will be gathered that the great points to be insisted upon in four-oared rowing are uniformity, and again uniformity, and always uniformity. A coach should insist, if possible even more strenuously than he insists in an Eight, on bodies and slides moving with a faultless precision and perfectly together. Let him devote his energies to getting the finish and recovery locked up all through the crew, and let him see to it that the movements of their bodies shall be slow and balanced on the forward swing, and strong and not jerky on the back swing. More it would be difficult to add.

When a Four is practising for a four-oared race alone – that is to say, when its members are not rowing in an eight-oared crew as well, their course of work should be similar to that laid down for an Eight. But when, as often happens at Henley, a Four is made up out of the members of an eight-oared crew, it will always be found better to allow its members to do the bulk of their work in the Eight, and to confine themselves in the Four principally to long and easy paddling, varied by short, sharp bursts of rowing. It may be necessary for such a Four to go over the full course once at top speed, but that ought to be enough. Their work in the Eight should get them into condition;

all that they really need in the Four is to be able to row perfectly together. The Brasenose Four that won the Stewards' in 1890 had never rowed over the full course before the day of the race. Their longest piece of rowing, as distinguished from paddling, had been a burst of three minutes. Their men acquired fitness by working in the Eight, and proved their condition by the two desperate races they rowed.

As to steering, it used to be said that anybody might steer in a Four except stroke, but Mr Guy Nickalls has proved that a stroke can steer as well as row. He has won four Stewards' Cup medals, has stroked and steered in every race, and his boat has always been kept on a faultless course.

In the case of the ordinary oar, however, the old saying, I think, holds good. Bow naturally is the best place to steer from, not only because in turning his head he can obtain a clear view of the course, but also because he has a considerable advantage in leverage, and ought to be able to control the direction of his boat merely by relaxing or increasing the power applied to his oar. The best part of the stroke for looking round is, I consider, towards the finish. A turn of the head, accompanied by an outward movement of the outside elbow to suit the slightly altered position of the body, while keeping pressure on the oar, is all that is necessary. Yet I have seen Mr Guy Nickalls look round in the middle of his forward swing without apparently disturbing the equilibrium of the boat. In any case, the best thing a steerer can do is to learn his course by heart, so that he may be able to steer for the most part without looking round at all, judging the direction she is taking by her stern and by well-known objects on the bank as he passes them. Personally I prefer, and I think most men prefer, to steer with the outside foot. The captain of a Four should always look carefully to his steering-gear to see that the wires and strings are taut, and that they move properly and without jamming over the wheels. I have seen more than one race lost by accidents to the steering-gear that might have been avoided by a little preliminary attention.

PAIR OARS

This, too, is a very pleasant form of rowing, both with a view to racing and merely for casual amusement. The main elements for success are similar to those laid down in the case of Fours. In pair-oared rowing, however, there is one important point which distinguishes it from all other forms of rowing. It is absolutely essential that the two men composing a Pair should not row "jealous," i.e. neither of them must attempt to row the other round in order to prove his own superior strength and ability. Such a course of action not only makes progress circuitous and slow, but also ends by entirely destroying the tempers of both oarsmen. In a Pair, even more than in a Four, the bow oar has a considerable advantage in leverage, whence it comes that a lighter and less powerful man can often row bow in a Pair with a strong and heavy stroke. The most surprising instance of this occurred in the Oxford University Pairs of 1891, which were won by the late Mr H. B. Cotton, rowing bow at 9 stone 12 lbs., to the stroke of Mr Vivian Nickalls, who weighed close on 13 stone. An instance to the contrary was afforded by the winners of the Goblets at Henley in 1878. These were Mr. T. C. Edwards-Moss, bow, 12 stone 3 lbs., and Mr W. A. Ellison, stroke, 10 stone 13 lbs. The Goblets at Henley have been won six times by Mr. Guy Nickalls, and five times by his brother Vivian.

SWIVEL ROWLOCKS

There has been, during the past year, a movement in favour of using swivel rowlocks, not only in sculling-boats, but also in Pairs, Fours, and Eights, though the majority of English oarsmen, even when inclined to use them in Pairs and Fours, set their faces against them for Eights. The advocates of swivels contend that by their use the hands are eased on the recovery, and the jar that takes place when the oar turns on a fixed rowlock is absolutely abolished. These advantages seem to me to be exaggerated, for, though I have carefully watched for it, I have never seen an Eight or a Four retarded in her place for even a fraction of a second by the supposed jar due to the turning of the oar on the feather in fixed rowlocks. On the other hand, I am convinced that for an ordinary eight-oared crew the fixed rowlock is best, and for the following reasons: –

The combined rattle of the oars as they turn constitutes a most valuable rallying-point. The ears are brought into action as well as the eyes. This advantage is lost with swivels. In modern sculling-boats a man must use swivels, for the reach of the sculler extends to a point which he could not reach with fixed rowlocks, as his sculls would lock before he got there. As he moves forward he is constantly opening up, his arms extending on either side of his body; but in rowing, one arm swings across the body, and unless you are going to screw the body round towards the rigger, and thus sacrifice all strength of beginning, you cannot fairly reach beyond a certain point, which is just as easily and comfortably attained with fixed rowlocks as with swivels. Moreover – and here is the great advantage – you have in the thole-pin of a fixed rowlock an absolutely immovable surface, and the point of application of your power is always the same throughout the stroke. With a swivel this is not so, for the back of the swivel, against which your oar rests, is constantly moving. To put it in other words, it is far easier with a fixed rowlock to get a square, firm, clean grip of the beginning, and for the same reason it is easier to bring your oar square and clean out at the end of the stroke. A really good waterman can, of course, adapt himself to swivels, as he can to almost anything else in a boat, but his task will not be rendered any easier by them. For average oars, and even for most good oars, the difficulties of rowing properly will be largely increased, without any compensating advantage, so far as I am able to judge. In the case of novices, I am convinced that it would be quite disastrous to attempt to make them row with swivel rowlocks.

Sculling

By Guy Nickalls.

In writing an article on sculling, a sculler must of necessity be egotistical. He can only speak of what he himself feels to be the correct way of doing things, and cannot judge of how a different man feels under the same circumstances. I therefore put in a preliminary plea for forgiveness if in the course of these remarks the letter 'I' should occur with excessive frequency. Sculling is so entirely an art by itself, that a man might just as well ask a painter how he produces an impression on a canvas as ask a sculler why he can scull, or how it comes that so many good oarsmen cannot scull. Ask an ordinary portrait-painter why he cannot sketch a landscape, and ask an ordinary oarsman to explain why he cannot scull, and to the uninitiated the answer of both will have the same sort of vagueness. Sculling differs so vastly from rowing that no man who has not tried his hand at both can appreciate how really wide apart they stand; and the fact that sculling depends to such a great extent on one's innate sense of touch and balance, makes it extremely hard for a man who has tried his hand with some success at both sculling and rowing to explain to the novice, or even to the veteran oarsman, wherein the difference lies. There is as much difference between sculling and rowing as there is between a single cyclist racing without pacemakers, steering and balancing himself and making his own pace, and a man in the middle of a quintette merely pedalling away like a machine at another man's pace, and not having the balance or anything else solely under his control. The difference in 'feel' is so great that one might liken it to the difference between riding a light, springy, and eager thoroughbred which answers quickly to every touch, and pounding uncomfortably along on a heavy, coarse-bred horse, responding slowly to an extra stimulus, and deficient in life and action.

To scull successfully one must possess pluck, stamina, and a cool head, and must, above all, be a waterman. A man may row well and successfully, and yet possess none of these qualities. Nothing depresses a man more when he is sculling than his sense of utter isolation. If a spurt is required, he alone has to initiate it and carry it through; there is no cheering prospect of another strong back aiding one, no strenuous efforts of others to which one can rally, no cox to urge one to further effort. You feel this even more in practice than in actual racing, especially when going against the clock. You are your own stroke, captain, crew, and cox, and success or failure depends entirely and absolutely upon yourself. No one else (worse luck) is to blame if things go wrong.

The pace of a sculling-boat is strictly proportionate to the quality of its occupant. A good man will go fast and win his race; a bad man cannot. A good man in an Eight cannot make his crew win; and a bad man in an Eight may mar a crew, but he can also very often win a race against a crew containing better men than himself.

People have often asked me why a first-class oar should not of necessity be a good sculler. This, although a hard matter to explain, is partly accounted for by what I have said above, in that sculling is so greatly a matter of delicate touch and handling. Even good oars are as often as not clumsy and wanting in a quick light touch. Very few really big men have ever been fine scullers. This is partly accounted for by the fact that so few boats are built large enough to carry big weights, and consequently they are under-boated when practising. Many big weights, e.g. S. D. Muttlebury and F. E. Churchill, have been good and fast scullers at Eton, but two or three years afterwards are slow, and get slower and slower the longer they continue. This, I think, is a good deal owing to the muscle which a big man generally accumulates, especially on the shoulders and arms, and he therefore lacks the essential qualities of elasticity, lissomness, and quickness with the hands.

Big, strong men also generally grip with great ferocity the handles of their sculls, and these being small, the forearm becomes cramped, and gives out. Many good oarsmen have never tried to scull, and those who have generally give it up after a first failure, which is more often than not due to want of attention to detail. What passes for good watermanship in an Eight is mere clumsiness in a sculling-boat, and, as a matter of fact, there are far fewer really good watermen than the casual observer imagines.

I asked three of our best modern heavyweight oarsmen to tell me the reason why they could not scull. The Thames RC man said the only reason why he had never won the Diamonds was because he had never gone in for them. This was straightforward, but unconvincing to anyone who had watched this gentleman gambolling in a sculling boat. The Cambridge heavyweight affirmed solemnly that he could scull, and was at one time very fast. He subsequently admitted that he could never get a boat big enough, and, secondly, his arms always gave. The Oxford heavyweight replied much to the same purpose, without the preliminary affirmation.

Many men can scull well and slowly, but few can really go fast, and this, I think, is due to the fact that they do not practise enough with faster men than themselves, and so do not learn by experience what action of theirs will best propel a boat at its fastest pace. Nothing is more deceptive than pace; when a man thinks he is going fastest he is generally going slowest. He gets the idea that he is going fast because his boat is jumping under him, and creating a large amount of side-wash; but an observer from the bank will notice that although the sculls are applying great power, that power is not being applied properly, and his boat will be seen to be up by the head and dragging at the stern, and bouncing up and down instead of travelling.

The first and foremost thing, then, to be attended to for pace is balance, i.e. an even keel, and to obtain this your feet should be very firm in your clogs. As those supplied by the trade are of a very rough and rudimentary character, they will nearly always require padding in different places. You should be able to feel your back stop just so much that when leaning back well past the perpendicular you can push hard against it with a straight leg. You are then quite firm, and can control your body in the event of your boat rolling. Although when a man has become a waterman he will find the back stop unnecessary, it is safest for the novice to have it, so as to be able to press against it; otherwise, having nothing to press against at the finish of his stroke, he may acquire the bad habit of relying entirely on his toes to pull him forward. In such a position he is unstable, and if his boat rolls he has no control over his body.

Having got your balance, the next thing to be thought of is the stroke. Reach forward until the knees touch either armpit; put the sculls in quite square, and take the water firmly (be most careful not to rush or jerk the beginning); at the same time drive with the legs, sending the slide, body and all, back; the loins must be absolutely firm, so that the seat does not get driven away from underneath the body. If you allow the loins to be loose and weak you will acquire that caterpillar action which was to be seen in several aspirants to Diamond Sculls honours last year, and which ruined whatever poor chance they ever possessed. This diabolical habit of driving the slide away, although common to many professionals, cannot be too severely condemned, as it relieves the sculler from doing any work at all except with the arms, which, if thus used, without swing and legwork to help them, cannot, unless a man is enormously muscular in them, hold out for any great length of time. The firm drive will start the swing of the body, which may be continued a fraction of time after the slide has finished. You will find that when you have driven your slide back your body will have swung well past the perpendicular (and in sculling you may swing further back than you are allowed to in rowing). When in that position a sculler is allowed to do that which an oarsman must not, viz. he may help to start his recovery by moving his body slightly up to meet his sculls as they finish the stroke. Thus by keeping his weight on the blades in the water as long as possible, instead of in his boat, he strengthens the finish and prevents his boat burying itself by the bows. The stroke from the beginning should go on increasing in strength to the finish, which should be firm and strong, but, like the beginning, not jerked or snapped. Strength applied to the finish keeps a boat travelling in between the strokes.

The finish is by far the hardest part of the stroke, and is most difficult to get clean and smart. The position is naturally a far weaker one than that of the oarsman, as the hands are eight inches or so further back, and at the same time six inches or so clear of the ribs. In this position nine out of ten scullers fail to get a really quick recovery with the sculls clean out and clear of the water, the hands away like lightning and clear of the knees, and the body at the same time swinging forward. As soon as the hands have cleared the knees they should begin to turn the blade off the feather, so that by the time you are full forward the blades are square and ready to take the water. Professionals recommend staying on the feather until just before the water is taken, but this is apt to make the novice grip his handles tightly, and press on them almost unconsciously when he should be very light. He will thus make his blade fly up and miss the beginning. In order to ensure both hands working perfectly level and taking and leaving the water exactly together, a man should watch his stern, and by the turn given either way he can easily detect which hand is not doing its right amount of work. Which hand you scull over or which under makes little or no difference. Personally, I scull with the right hand under. In holding a scull the thumb should 'cap' the handle; this prevents you from pulling your button away from the thowl even the slightest bit, and makes your grip firmer and steadier. If in steering you must look right round, do so shortly before you are full forward, as soon as the hands have cleared the knees, but generally steer by the stern, if you can, without looking round, and almost unconsciously by what you notice out of the corner of either eye as you pass.

Modern professionals, with very few exceptions, scull in disgracefully bad form. W. Haines, Wag Harding, and W. East, at his best, are perhaps the only exceptions I know to this rule. English professionals, owing to the manual labour with which most of them start life, become abnormally strong in the arms, and trust almost entirely to those muscles. Their want of swing, their rounded backs, and 'hoicked' finish they carry with them into a rowing boat. Nothing shows up their bad form in rowing so much as sandwiching a few pros. in a goodish amateur crew – 'by their style ye shall know them.' They have acquired a style which does not answer, and which they cannot get rid of, and they consider an Eight can be propelled in the same manner as a sculling boat. Nothing is more erroneous. They cannot assimilate their style to the correct one. Two pros sometimes make a fair pair, because they may happen to 'hoick' along in the same style. Professional Fours are a little worse than Pairs, and their Eights disgraceful. I am of opinion (and I fancy most men who know anything about rowing will agree with me) that England's eight best amateurs in a rowing boat would simply lose England's eight best pros over any course from a mile upwards. This inability to assimilate one's style to that of another man, or body of men, may be the reason why some excellent amateur scullers proved inferior oars, or it may be that they can go at their own pace and not at another man's. I myself have often felt on getting out of a sculling boat into an Eight great difficulty and much weariness at being compelled to go on at another man's pace, and only too easy at another's order. If you are practising for sculling as well as rowing there is nothing like being captain of an Eight or stroke of a Pair or Four.

The novice, if he has toiled so far as this, is no doubt by now saying to himself that I am only repeating what he knows already, and that what he especially requires are hints as to rigging his boat, size and shape of sculls, and various measurements, the pace of stroke he ought to go, etc., Of course, the smaller the blade the quicker the stroke, and vice versa. It should be remembered that even ¹⁄₁₆ of an inch extra in the breadth of a blade makes a lot of difference. Blades, I think, should vary according to the liveliness of water rowed on, and according to the strength of the individual. For myself, I am rather in favour of smaller blades than are generally used. My experience leads me to believe that racing sculls should be from 9 feet 8½ inches to 9 feet 9½ inches in length all over; in-board measurement from 2 feet 8¼ inches to 2 feet 9 inches, but, of course, this entirely depends on how much you like your sculls to overlap. When they are at right angles to the boat, my sculls overlap so much that there is a hand's-breadth of space in between my crossed hands. The length of blade should be about 2 feet; breadth of blade, from 5¾ inches to 6¼ inches. Even on the tideway sculls should be as light as a good scull-maker can turn them out, so long as they retain their stiffness. Do not, however, sacrifice stiffness to lightness. It is rather interesting to compare these measurements with those of a pair of sculls hanging over my head as I write; these were used in a championship race eighty years ago, and have a heavy square loom to counteract their length and consequent weight out-board. The measurements are – 8 feet 8 inches in length over all, 1 foot 9 inches in-board; length of blade, 2 feet 5 inches.; breadth of blade, 3⅛ inches. I give below roughly what should be the measurements of a boat according to the weight of the sculler. For a man of –

	9 stone	12 stone	13 stone
Length	30 feet	31 feet	31 feet 3 inches
Width	9 inches	10½ inches	11½ inches
Depth	5¼ inches	5½ inches	5¾ inches
Depth forward	3¼ inches	3½ inches	3⅝ inches
Depth aft	2½ inches	2½ inches	2⅝ inches
Weight	24 lbs	28 lbs	34 lbs

As to slide, I hold that a man should slide to a point level with his rowing-pin – never past it, lest the boat should be pinched instead of being driven at the beginning of the stroke.

The clogs should be fixed at an angle of 55° to the keel (i.e. an angle measured along the back of the clogs). If the angle is much smaller, the feet and legs lose power when the sculler is full back, and the drive at the finish is weakened. If the angle is greater, the difficulty of bending the ankle-joints sufficiently as the slide moves forward becomes very serious. The distance of fifteen inches from the heel of the clogs to the edge of slide when full forward may be slightly reduced, but only slightly. For instance, if reduced, as is sometimes done, to ten inches, the body comes too close to the heels in the forward position to enable the sculler to get a strong, direct, and immediate drive, and the boat is pinched.

A very old sculling boat of mine – and perhaps the best that Clasper ever built – was built for Mr F. I. Pitman in 1886. She owed her pace to the fact that she was very long aft, and consequently never got up by the head; her cutwater was always in the water, even when her occupant was full forward; and the most marvellous thing was that, low as she was, she did not bury her nose, considering that she had to endure a weight of 170 lbs or so, shifting its position fore and aft to the extent of sixteen inches. She is a marvel of the boatbuilder's art, and was built of exceptionally close-framed cedar, which takes a long time to get water-soaked, and indeed should never do so if properly looked after. Her dimensions were: Length, 31 feet 2 inches.; length from edge of sliding seat when forward to stern-post, 14 feet 6½ inches; width, 11¼ inches.; depth forward, 3¼ inches; depth aft, 2⅝ inches; depth amidships, 5½ inches; from heels to back edge of slide when back, 3 feet 5¼ inches; leverage, i.e. measurement from thowl to thowl across, 4 feet 9 inches; from heels to edge of seat when forward, 15¼ inches. She won the Diamond Sculls in 1886, 1888, 1889, 1890; the amateur championship in 1886, 1887, 1888, 1889, 1890; besides the Metropolitan Sculls and several minor races.

It is a great mistake to try and get a boat too light. The eagerness a man will display in cutting down everything to lessen the weight of his craft, until he is sitting on the water on a weak bit of nothing, is really astounding. Three or four extra pounds often make all the difference, whether a boat is stiff and keeps on travelling, or whether she jumps, cocks her head, and waggles about generally.

As to the pace of stroke, from twenty-two to twenty-six strokes a minute is a fair practice paddle, twenty-four to twenty-eight for sculling hard, and in racing, even for a minute, never attempt anything over thirty-eight. I once sculled seventy-eight strokes in two minutes, and felt more dead than alive at the end of it. It is harder work to scull thirty-eight strokes in a minute than it is to row forty-four in the same time. If you do start at thirty-eight, drop down as soon as possible to thirty-four, thirty-two, or even thirty, according to circumstances of wind and weather, etc. My best advice to the novice is to go just fast enough to clean out his opponent before the same thing happens to himself, or, even better still, to get his opponent beaten, and leave himself fresh. But always remember if you are at all evenly matched, that however bad you feel yourself, your opponent is probably in just as bad a plight. Talking of pace reminds me of how soon even the best scullers tire. In sculling a course against time at Henley, a good man may get to Fawley, the halfway point, in about the same time as a Pair, and yet will be half a minute slower from that point to the finish; and for the last quarter-mile the veriest tiro can out-scull a champion, provided the latter has gone at his best pace throughout. In scull-racing the advantage of the lead is greater than in rowing, as a sculler can help his own steering by watching the direction of the other's craft. Yet you should never sacrifice your wind to obtain the advantage, for recollect that in sculling you can never take a blow or an easy for even a stroke. If you are behind, never turn round to look at your opponent, as by doing so you lose balance and pace, and many a good man has lost a race by so doing. Keep just so close up to your man as to prevent him giving you the disadvantage of his back wash.

Training for sculling requires more time and practice than training for rowing. If it takes an Eight six weeks to get together and fit to race, it takes a Four nine weeks, a Pair twelve weeks, and a Sculler fifteen weeks. If a man is training for both rowing and sculling at the same time, and racing in both on the same day, it takes lengths and lengths off his pace, for rowing upsets all that precision so necessary in sculling. If a man sculls and rows at Henley, and does both on the same day, and practises for the same daily for a month beforehand, I should think it would make him from six to eight lengths slower on the Henley course. Otherwise, train as you would for rowing, the only difference being that a little more time should be spent in the actual sculling than is spent in the actual rowing.

Having attended Henley Regatta since 1883, and having raced there for twelve years in succession, I have met with various scullers. Mr J. C. Gardner, taking him all round, was the finest I have ever seen of amateurs. He was quite the best stripped man I have ever seen, his muscles standing out like bars of steel all over his body; he was a very neat, finished sculler, the only fault I could find with him being a tendency to a weak finish. W. S. Unwin, a light weight, was extremely neat, but his style was rather spoilt by a roundish back. F. I. Pitman, his great rival, was perhaps a better stayer, and had a more elegant style. Vivian Nickalls, for a long man, was a fine sculler, handicapped by an awkward finish and handicapped also by the fact that he never entirely gave his time up to sculling only – his chief characteristic being a fine, healthy, long body swing. M. Bidault, a Frenchman, who rowed in the Metropolitan Regatta some years ago, was 7 feet 4½ inches high; he weighed 17 stone; his boat weighed 50 lbs, was 35 feet long, had a 5 feet leverage; his sculls were 11 feet 10 inches long. Compare with him Wag Harding, with a boat 19½ lbs in weight, weighing 9 stone himself, and you will see in what different forms and shapes men can scull. And M. Bidault was a fast man for a quarter of a mile. The fastest sculler for half a mile I have ever seen was Herr Doering, who sculled for the Diamonds in 1887. The slowest man I have ever seen was – well, I won't mention names, as he might go in for the Diamond Sculls again. Rupert Guinness, although not what I should call a born sculler, obtained his great proficiency in sculling by dint of a very long and careful preparation, by months and months of continual practice, and by not hampering his sculling by entering and practising for rowing events at the same time – in fact, by making a speciality of sculling.

Steering
(Some Hints to
Novice Coxswains)

By G. L. Davis

Many people think that any one, provided he be of the proper weight, is fitted to fill the post of coxswain.

Nobody, however, knows better than the actual rowing man what an amount of useless labour and irritation a crew can be saved by possessing a good man in the stern, not to mention the assistance he can afford both directly and indirectly in getting a crew together. Certainly a mere tiro, having acquired the elementary knowledge that if he pulls the right rudder line he will turn his boat to starboard, i.e. to the right, and that if he pulls his left line he will turn her to port, i.e. to the left, may be able to guide a boat sufficiently well for ordinary purposes; but even in the period of training a crew, and still more so in the race, there is undoubtedly plenty of scope for a clever coxswain to distinguish himself. There is no royal road to good steering. Pains and perseverance are necessary, as in every other branch of athletics. The attainment of perfection in steering is not all that is requisite; there are many other qualities added to this skill which combine to make a coxswain worthy to be reckoned in the front rank – a position which all coxswains should aim for.

In the days of Tom Egan the steerer had to act as coach to his crew, but nowadays he is no longer called upon to do so. He is, in the first place, chosen on account of his light weight; but eligible though he may be in this respect, he is too often quite incapable in other ways of performing his duties. Should this be the case, a crew would be well advised in carrying a few more pounds, or even a stone or two extra, if by so doing they manage to gain an able and experienced coxswain. There are certain qualities which are absolutely essential in the right sort. He should have light hands, judgment, a cool head, and plenty of nerve to enable him to keep his presence of mind in the face of a sudden predicament or unforeseen danger. There are numberless occasions both in practice and during races when risks are run. A boat laden with pleasure seekers may suddenly pop out from the bank into the course. The coolness of the coxswain may avert very much more serious consequences than the loss of a stroke or two, such as a broken rigger or an injury to an oarsman, by a touch of the rudder and a ready appeal to his crew to mind their oars.

During a University Boat Race, in which I was steering the Cambridge Boat, a waterman's wherry, with two or three occupants, was suddenly pulled out from the Surrey shore at a short distance above Hammersmith Bridge. The course at this point lies somewhat near to the bank, and the Oxford Boat was nearly level with mine. The wherry was directly in my way, and, as far as I could make out, those who were in it seemed to be in doubt as to whether they should row still further out or make for the shore. If I went to the right, a foul was imminent with the Oxford Boat; if to the left, I should have got into slack water and lost ground by the detour. There was no time for those in the wherry to waste in making up their minds, so I promptly made straight for them with the object of driving them out of my course. The desired effect followed. They got sufficient way on in the direction of the shore to enable me to steer straight on and clear them. My action involved the ticklish question of judgment of distance and of pace, namely, should I reach the spot before the wherry was clear; and this anecdote illustrates my point – that quickness in making up the mind, and, when it is made up, in acting, is essential to a coxswain.

The duties of a coxswain consist of many and varied details. To make a smart crew, attention should be paid to discipline both in and out of the boat, and he can and ought to further this object to the utmost of his power, thereby saving the coach or captain a great deal of trouble. If the coxswain of a light eight-oared racing ship has been ordered to get her into the water, he ought to be there to superintend the order being carried out. He should bid his crew 'stand by' their riggers, and see that each man is in readiness to lift and carry her to the water's edge. There is generally a waterman at hand, but whether there is or not, the coxswain should be ready, if necessary, to remove any stool upon which the ship may have been resting, so as to prevent any stumbling on the part of his men. His place is near the rudder (unless she is launched stern foremost, when, of course, it would be impossible), to prevent any injury happening to it, until the boat is safely in the water. He will then get the oarsmen into her in an orderly manner. There is necessity for this, for otherwise the boat's back may be strained. This might occur by allowing stroke and bow to get in first, owing to a boat of such length and lightness of build being supported in the centre and at the same time weighted at each end. The best order for the men to take their places is, 4, 5, 3, 6, 2, 7, bow, and then stroke. The coxswain should call out their numbers one by one, holding the boat firmly while they take their seats, and on no account allow more than one man to get in at the same time. In disembarking, it is part of his duty to see that the crew leave the ship in the reverse order. The coxswain seats himself in the aftermost thwart perfectly upright, with his legs crossed tailor-fashion, and takes up the rudder lines one in each hand; and, before he gives any command, should see that his steering gear is in proper order. It is a common and useful custom for the purpose of preventing the hand from slipping, to have attached to each line a piece of wood of about three to four inches in length, and one and a half in circumference, called a tug. These the coxswain clasps tightly, one in each hand. Some coxswains hold their rudder lines in front of the body, others behind; but in my opinion the best place to hold them is by the side, with the hands resting one on each gunwale. The coxswain, by thus supporting himself, can better preserve a firm and steady seat. He should never slip about on his seat, but always keep his body as nearly as possible erect, and balanced from his hips. He must on no account roll with the boat, and should endeavour to prevent himself being moved to and fro by the action of the rowers. Often a narrow strip of wood is nailed to the seat the better to enable him to sit firm. The lines must be kept taut, and tied together in front of him, lest by any accident he should lose one or both overboard. After having shoved off and paddled into position, he should see that the bows of his boat point straight for the course he wishes to steer. He will then start his crew by calling upon them to 'get ready,' when they will divest themselves of any superfluous clothing and make any other necessary preparations. He will then say 'Forward!' or 'Forward all!' for them to come forward in readiness for the first stroke. He should now take care that his boat is level, and should tell the oarsmen on the side to which she may list to raise their hands, or call upon the crew to get her level. After that he asks, 'Are you ready?' as a final warning, and lastly cries, 'Row!' or 'Paddle!' as may be required. Some other forms are employed, but this is as good as any, and better than most, and the same words should always be used when once adopted. In the event of a crew making a bad start, they should be at once stopped and restarted. If the coxswain be desirous for his crew to stop rowing or paddling, 'Easy all!' is the term to use, and this order should be given almost immediately after the commencement of a stroke, to prevent the rowers coming forward for the next one. In case it may be necessary to bring his boat up sharp, he will say, 'Hold her up all!' and if (at any time) there is any danger of the oars touching anything, he should cry, 'Mind your oars, bow side,' or 'stroke side,' as the case may be. The boat is ordinarily turned on the port (left) side by calling upon bow and No. 3 to paddle, and stroke and No. 6 to back water, or back, for brevity; and on the starboard (right) side by calling upon Nos. 2 and 4 to paddle, and Nos. 5 and 7 to back. In each case the coxswain naturally assists with the rudder. When turning a racing ship, for fear of weakening her, the paddling and rowing should not take place simultaneously.

Whatever the coxswain addresses to his crew should be spoken clearly and distinctly, so that all may hear without difficulty. The preceding instructions comprise most of the everyday terms that a coxswain should know.

Now let me turn to his functions of a semi-coaching character, of keeping his crew in time. Whether the crew are rowing or paddling, he must carefully watch the time of the oars, both as they catch the water and leave it. If the oarsman catches the water too soon, he should be told not to hurry; if too late, he should be told, 'You're late.' If he leaves it too soon, or, as it is called, clips his stroke at the finish, he should be told to finish it out, etc. (but if an oarsman finishes it after the stroke, I cannot advise the coxswain to take notice of it). All these semi-coaching remarks, if I may so call them, should be prefaced with the number of the crew to whom they are addressed, for the purpose of calling his attention, and must be used with judgment and tact, for nothing can be more aggravating, not to say maddening, to an oarsman at any time, more especially when fagged in a race, to hear incessantly the possibly high-pitched and monotonous tones of a coxswain. There is only one fault that will excuse him shouting himself hoarse, if he be so disposed, and it is the fault, or rather vice, of one of the crew looking out of the boat; and he should at once cry, 'Eyes in the boat!' and continue to do so until he is obeyed. There are certain acts of watermanship which an efficient coxswain will not neglect to carry out, namely, when turning to come downstream, to swing his boat round by pulling her head outwards into the current; and, on the other hand, when turning to proceed upstream, to thrust her nose into the slack water inshore, and allow her stern to come round in the same manner; and always to bring his boat in to the raft or landing stage with her head pointing upstream.

There is no need for me to set out the rules of the road for a coxswain to follow, as they can be read at any time in the Rowing Almanack, which comes out annually, and is published at the Field office.

To steer a straight course, a coxswain should fix upon a high and conspicuous object some distance ahead, and endeavour to keep the nose of his boat dead on it; and when learning his course, he should remember to choose objects of a permanent nature, or in the race he will be in difficulties. Now, the keeping of a straight course is not as simple as it appears; in fact, it is a most difficult thing to do properly, and there is no case in which the advantage of a coxswain with light hands is better displayed. It will be noticed that such a one leaves scarcely a ripple in his wake, while another will leave a considerable wash. The reason of it is this: that while the former uses practically no rudder, the latter, by first pulling one line and then the other, causes the stern of his boat to swing from side to side, until, as the sailors say, she becomes wild – that is to say, so unsteady that the further she travels the more rudder she will require to prevent her bows from yawing and to keep her course. He should never steer for a curve in the bank or for other projections – as, for instance, the buttress of a bridge – in such a manner as to be compelled to sheer out to clear them. He should approach a sharp corner as wide as possible, in order to reduce the acuteness of the angle at which he will have to take it, and should have the boat's head round by the time that the axis or pivot, if I may use the term, on which the boat swings, and which in the eight-oared boats I steered was usually trimmed to be somewhere between the seats of Nos. 4 and 5, is off the most prominent point.

The difficulty of taking this sort of corner is increased when the course lies up-stream, according to the strength of the current; for not only does the current acting on the bows tend to prevent the boat coming round, but also to drive her head towards the opposite bank. When the Cam at Cambridge is in flood, 'Grassy' and Ditton are corners of this character, but usually that river runs sluggishly. But even then these corners present many difficulties. 'Grassy' is on the right bank of the river, and therefore on the coxswain's left; Ditton is on his right. The former is the harder to manipulate properly, by reason of the river becoming a narrow neck shortly before the corner is reached.

In taking 'Grassy,' the coxswain should keep close to the tow-path bank until he commences to make the turn. It is impossible to explain on paper the exact spot when he should do so. The common fault is to begin too soon. Practice and experience only can teach him when to time his action correctly; but having acquired this knowledge, he will get his boat round with but a moderate amount of rudder, especially if he calls upon bow and No. 3 for a little extra assistance.

Some years ago, during the Lent Term Bumping Races at Cambridge, the coxswain of one of the boats, with the intention of cutting off the preceding one as it was being steered round in the correct way, took this very corner close to the inside bend at its very commencement, and in so doing acted contrary to the principle of giving a sharp corner a wide berth at the first part. The consequence was that, having failed to calculate the pace at which the other was travelling, and having missed his bump, he found it impossible to bring his boat round, ran high and dry on to the opposite bank, and was, of course, himself bumped.

Ditton should be approached as wide as the coxswain can manage, by hugging the opposite bank until he begins to bring the boat's head round, which, as in the case of Grassy, should not be done until as late as possible. Here, too, Nos 2 and 4 may be called upon to help her round. The rudder should be put on between the strokes as a rule, gradually, and not with a jerk, which has a tendency to cause the boat to roll. It should be used as lightly as possible, and never under ordinary circumstances put hard on. The effect of a cross wind is to drive the stern of a boat to leeward, and to bring her bows up into the wind. This should be counteracted by the coxswain steering to windward of his usual course, and by Lee Rudder to meet her: how much can only be learnt by experience, and must be regulated by the strength of the wind. The fin, which is a thin plate of metal fixed slightly abaft the coxswain's seat on her keelson, is of great assistance in keeping the boat straight under such circumstances.

The coxswain should pick up information relating to his course by observation, inquiries, and in every way he can, and, previous to a race, he should take careful stock of the direction and force of the wind, and shape his course accordingly. It is a good plan to be taken over the course either in a row boat or launch, by someone acquainted with it, for the purposes of instruction. He can gain a general idea of the Putney to Mortlake course by watching the barges which float up and down the river with the tide, and are kept in midstream by long sweeps. But every coxswain should learn to scull; he can then not only get his weight down by exercise, if required, but familiarize himself with the set of the stream, flats, and other peculiarities of a course by actual experience. Training for the purpose of reducing the weight of the coxswain is a questionable expedient; but if practised with moderation, and if natural means are employed, the object, if worth it – which I very much doubt –may be attained, and little harm done; but weakness, the result of excessive wasting, is not unfrequently accompanied with an impaired judgment and loss of nerve, the absence of which may lead to serious consequences. Moreover, a coxswain not only requires a certain amount of physical strength to manage a boat of the length of an eight oar, but, to do himself justice, should come to the post feeling full of energy and determination. In level races the coxswain of the leading boat should never take his opponents' water, unless reasonably certain that he cannot be overtaken, for a sudden sheer out involving loss of pace and ground at a critical time has before now lost a race; and when alongside, and in close proximity, he should avoid watching the other boat, otherwise he will in all probability steer into it, such is the apparent force of attraction exercised over a coxswain by the opposing crew. One coxswain should not 'bore' the other. Boring is the act of one coxswain steering closer and closer to another until he gradually succeeds in pushing him out of his own water. This cannot take place when both coxswains engaged are equally skilful, and equally well acquainted with the course, for neither will give way. At the best it is not sportsmanlike, and there is no desire on the part of the majority of rowing men to win a race by the trickery of the coxswains. At the annual University Boat Race Dinner, when the old Blues and other friends assemble to do honour to the two crews, it is the time-honoured custom to drink the health of the coxswains. On one of these occasions, a well-known Oxford coxswain, who, in the fog that prevailed at the start of the race, had been pressed out of his course by the opposing crew, in returning thanks made a witty allusion to the subject in these words: 'I have been,' he said, 'very much interested in this race, but I have also been very much bored.' It was a speech meant for the occasion, and was received with the applause it deserved; but it was not meant seriously, nor was it taken so by his equally well-known Cambridge rival.

I may at this point give a word of advice to a coxswain in a Bumping Race. He should, throughout the race, keep his true course, and not follow any vagaries of the boat in front of him, except with the immediate object of making his bump; he must never shoot for his bump when going round a corner, and ought always to make sure of his position before making a shot, so as not to waste the energy of his men by missing time after time, and zigzagging across the river. When he has been bumped, or has made a bump, he should at once clear out of the way to make room for the boats following. In all races he should encourage his crew at intervals with such expressions as, 'Now, you fellows! Well rowed! On to it!' etc. But an incessant flow of language not only sounds ridiculous, but must be a nuisance to the crew themselves. In a ding-dong race, however, when neither crew can get away from the other, he will naturally urge them more strenuously to further exertions. He should watch the time as carefully as in practice, and call upon his crew to 'Reach out,' or 'Keep it long,' if he notices that they are getting short and scratchy; and he may quietly keep the stroke posted up in the doings of the opponents, telling him how they are rowing, how far ahead they are, and so on. In training quarters, especially if the crew are despondent, the more depressed they are, the more he should endeavour to cheer them up and inspire confidence in them.

Finally, let me advise coxswains when steering to wear warm and waterproof clothing in cold and wet weather, and thus possibly save themselves much suffering from rheumatism and other complaints in afterlife.

College Rowing
At Oxford

By C. M. Pitman
New College; President O.U.B.C. 1895.

A bump in the Eights.

If we try to examine the causes of success or failure, of a run of good crews or bad crews from one university or the other, it is impossible to overestimate the importance of good organization, good management, and friendly rivalry in the college boat clubs. In the long run, the success or failure of the University Crew depends in no small measure upon the amount of trouble taken and the amount of keenness shown by the various colleges in practising for their different races during the year. It is only by very careful coaching and assiduous practice in his college Torpid and Eight, that a man who has not rowed before going up to the University can ever hope to attain to a place in the University Crew; and it is only by trying to apply his learning to advantage in college races during the year that one who has just gained his blue can hope to be of greater value to the university in the following spring.

A BUMP IN THE EIGHTS

Only a small number of the men who take up rowing at the university attain to a seat in the Trial Eights, and fewer still, of course, get their blue. It is by rowing for their college, then, in Eight or Torpid, which the majority of university men gain their experience, and so it is but natural that even more interest is usually manifested in the practice of the Eights than in that of the University Crew itself.

Most of the colleges at Oxford have now what is known as an 'amalgamated club,' which supplies the finances of all the various branches of athletics. That is to say, every undergraduate member of the college pays a fixed subscription to the amalgamated club fund, and the money thus collected is allotted proportionately to the different college clubs. The money thus allotted, with the addition in some cases of small sums received as entrance fees for college races, forms the income of the college boat club; and out of this income is paid a capitation fee to the University Boat Club, which varies according to the number of undergraduates on the college books, the rest of the money being devoted to providing boats, oars, etc. – the ordinary expenses, in fact, for carrying on the college boat club.

A freshman, when he first comes up to Oxford, has, as a rule, made up his mind to which particular branch of athletics he intends to devote himself. If he intends to play football, and does not happen to have come up with a great reputation from his public school, he finds it somewhat hard at first, however good he may be, to make himself known; but if he makes up his mind to row, he finds everything cut and dried for him.

At the beginning of the October Term, a notice is put up for the benefit of freshmen and others that those desirous of being coached must be at the barge on and after a certain day, at 2.30 p.m. The coaching is undertaken by any of the college Eight of the preceding term who are in residence, and any others whom the captain of the boat club may consider qualified. The men are taken out at first in tub-pairs or heavy fours; and grotesque, to say the least of it, are the movements of the average freshmen during the first few days of his rowing career. The majority of men who get into a boat for the first time in their lives seem to imagine that it is necessary to twist their bodies into the most uncomfortable and unnatural it positions, and is hard at first to persuade them that the movements of a really good oar are easy, natural, and even graceful. It is not long, however, as a rule, before a considerable improvement becomes manifest, and, at the end of the first fortnight or so of the term, most of the novices have begun to get a grasp of the first principles of the art.

About the end of the second week of the term the freshmen are picked up into Fours. These crews, which row in heavy tub boats, practise for about three weeks for a race, which is rowed during the fifth or sixth week of the term. After a day or two of rest, the best men from these Fours are taken out in eights. No one who has not rowed in an eight with a crew composed almost entirely of beginners can imagine the discomfort, I might almost say the agony, of these first two or three rows. One of the chief causes of this is that the boats used on such occasions are usually, from motives of economy, very old ones, the riggers being often twisted and bent by the crabs of former generations, and the boats themselves heavy and inclined to be waterlogged.

During the last day or two of the term, the captain, with a view to making up his Torpids for the next term, generally tries to arrange one or two crews selected from the best of the freshmen and such of the old hands as are available; and justly proud is a freshman if, having got into a boat for the first time at the beginning of the term, he finds himself among the select few for the first Torpid at the end of it.

At the beginning of the Lent Term the energies of the college boat clubs are entirely devoted to the selection and preparation of the crews for the Torpids. The smaller colleges have one crew and the larger ones two, and in some cases three, crews each. No one who has rowed in his college Eight in the races of the previous summer is permitted to row in the Torpid, so the crews are generally composed partly of men who rowed in the Torpid of the preceding year, but who were not quite good enough to get into the Eight, and partly of freshmen; the boats used must be clinker built of five streaks, with a minimum beam measurement of 2 feet 2 inches measured inside, and with fixed seats.

Although I do not propose here to say anything about the general subject of training, I cannot refrain from making one remark. It is in practising for the Torpids that freshmen generally get their first experience of strict training, and for this reason there is no crew more difficult to train than a Torpid. Most of the men after their first experience of regular work have fine healthy appetites, and, as a rule, eat about twice as much as is good for them, with the result that, even if they escape violent indigestion, they are painfully short-winded, and find the greatest difficulty in rowing a fast stroke. The Torpids train for about three weeks before the races, which take place at the end of the fourth and the fifth weeks in term. They last for six nights, and are bumping races, the boats starting 160 feet apart. A 160 feet is a very considerable distance to make up in about three quarters of a mile, and at the head of a division a crew must be about fifteen seconds faster over the course to make certain of a bump.

Of performances in the Torpids that of Brasenose stands by itself. They finished at the head of the river in 1885, and remained there for eleven years, until they were displaced by New College in 1896.

The only other race in the Lent Term is the Clinker Fours. This race is rowed in sliding-seat clinker-built boats, and the crews consist of men who have not rowed in the Trial Eights or in the first division of the Eights in the previous Summer Term. For some occult reason there is never a large entry for the Clinker Fours, although the race affords an excellent opportunity of seeing how the best of the Torpid men row on slides, and should thus be a great help to the captain of a college boat club in making up his Eight for the next term. With so small an entry for the Clinker Fours, most of the college

Lent Races in the Plough Reach.

captains devote their time after the Torpids, for the rest of the term, to coaching their men in sliding-seat tubs, the time at the beginning of the Summer Term being so short that it is absolutely necessary to get the men who have been rowing on fixed seats in the Torpids thoroughly accustomed to slides by the end of the Lent Term, and also to have the composition of the next term's Eight as nearly as possible settled.

LENT RACES IN THE PLOUGH REACH

At the beginning of the Summer Term, time, as I have said, is rather short, and consequently it is the custom at most colleges to make the Eight come into residence about a week before the end of the vacation. The esprit de corps and energy which are shown during the practice are, perhaps, the most noticeable features of college rowing at Oxford – a circumstance to which may be attributed the fact that the crews turned out by the colleges at the top of the river are often wonderfully good, considering the material out of which they are formed. The Eights are rowed at the end of the fourth week and at the beginning of the fifth week in term, six nights in all. They start 130 foot apart – that is to say, 30 feet less than the Torpids. About the same number of boats row in a division in the former as in the latter, the bottom boat starting at the same place

A start in the Eights.

in each case; consequently the head boat in the Eights has a slightly longer course to row than the head Torpid.

The start of a boat race is always rather nervous work for the crews, but the start of a bumping race is worse in this respect than any. A spectator who cares to walk down the bank and look at the crews waiting at their posts for the start cannot fail to notice that even the most experienced men look extremely uncomfortable.

A START IN THE EIGHTS

The start is managed thus: at the starting-point of each boat a short wooden post is driven firmly into the ground. These posts are exactly 130 feet apart, and to each is attached a thin rope 60 feet long with a bung at the end, while by each post a punt is moored. About twenty minutes or a quarter of an hour before the appointed time, the crews start from their barges and paddle gently down to their respective starting places, where they take up their positions alongside of the punts. Five minutes before the starting-time the first gun is fired as a sort of warning. These guns are fired punctually to the second, and by the first gun the men who are going to start the different crews set their stopwatches. The duty of these 'starters' is to keep the crews informed of the exact time, by calling out, 'One minute gone,' 'Two minutes gone,' etc. The second gun goes one minute before the start, and as soon as it is fired, the waterman slowly pushes the boat out from the side of the punt by means of a long pole pressed against stroke's rigger, the coxswain holding the bung at arm's-length in his left hand, with the cord taut so as to counteract the pressure of the pole, and 'bow' and 'two' paddling very gently so as to keep the boat at the very furthest extension of the rope. 'Thirty seconds more,' calls the starter; 'fifteen,' 'ten,' 'five,' 'four,' 'three,' 'two,' 'look out' – Bang! and, except for those who are doomed to be bumped, the worst is over till the next night. Directly a bump is made both the boat which has made the bump and the boat which is bumped draw to one side, and on the next night the boat which has made the bump starts in front of its victim of the preceding evening. The Eights are the last event of the season in which the colleges compete against one another on the river, and the interest and excitement of the college in the doings of its crew generally find their final outlet, in the case of a college which has made five or six bumps or finished head of the river, in a bump supper – an entertainment of a nature peculiar to Oxford and Cambridge, which is, perhaps, better left to the imagination than described in detail.

It is a curious fact that, although the ideal aimed at by each college is the same, different colleges seem to adhere, to a very considerable extent, year after year to the same merits and the same faults. One college gets the reputation of not being able to row a fast enough stroke; another, of being ready to race a week before the races and of getting worse as the races proceed, and, try as hard as they like, they do not seem to be able to shake off the effect of the reputation of their predecessors. So, again, one college gets the reputation of rowing better in the races than could possibly be expected from their form in practice, or of always improving during the races. The most notable case of late years, perhaps, was the traditional pluck of Brasenose. For eleven years in the Torpids and for three years in the Eights their certain downfall was predicted, but year after year, sometimes by the skin of their teeth and sometimes with ease, they managed to get home. The best performances in the Eights, as a matter of mere paper record, are those of Trinity and Magdalen, who have each rowed head of the river for four years in succession, the former in 1861, 1862, 1863, and 1864, and the latter in 1892, 1893, 1894, and 1895. Magdalen can also boast of not having finished lower than third in the Eights for some fifteen years. Brasenose have finished head of the river fourteen times since the races were started in 1836; University nine times, and Magdalen seven times. The best performance in any one year is that of New College in the season 1895–96, when they completely swept the board, being head of the river in Eights and Torpids, and winning the University Fours, Pairs, and Sculls. The only other college race besides those I have described is the Fours. This race is rowed in coxswainless racing ships during the fourth week of the October Term. It is a 'time' race, the crews, which row two in a heat, starting eighty yards apart, the finishing posts being, of course, divided by the same distance. A time race is a very unsatisfactory affair compared with an ordinary 'breast' race, but it is rendered necessary by the narrow winding river, for there is not room between Iffley and Oxford for two boats to row abreast. Oxford College crews, undoubtedly excellent though they often are, have been singularly unsuccessful at Henley. The Grand Challenge Cup has only been won by a college crew from Oxford twice within the memory of the present generation (i.e. by Exeter, in 1882, and by New College in the present year). Wadham, it is true, won it in almost prehistoric times (1849), and the tradition is handed down that they took the light blue in their colours from those of the crew which they defeated – a tradition which I need hardly say the members of the sister University always meet with a most emphatic denial.

It may, perhaps, seem that so far I have described college rowing as if its organization were so perfect that there is little or no difficulty in managing a college boat club successfully. This is by no means the case. Uneasy lies the head that wears a crown, even though it be merely that of the captaincy of a college boat club.

In the first place, it is not always as easy as might be imagined to get men to row. Men who cannot be induced to row when they come up to the university may be divided into two classes – those who refuse because they do not wish to take up any branch of athletics, and those who will not row because they wish to do something else. The former class (i.e. those of them who, after a moderate amount of persuasion, will not come down to the river) are not, as a rule, worth bothering about. They are generally weak, soft creatures, whose highest ambition is to walk overdressed about the 'High,' and, if possible, to be considered 'horsey' without riding – the class, in fact, generally known as 'bloods.' Or else they belong to that worthy class of beings who come up to the university to read and only to read, and imagine that it is therefore impossible for them to row. The 'blood' is, or should be, beneath the contempt of the rowing authorities, and the 'bookworm' is generally impervious to argument, in spite of the fact that he would be able to read much harder if he took regular exercise.

With regard, however, to those men who refuse to row because they want to go in for something else, a little diplomacy and a little personal trouble on the part of the college captain, such as coaching men at odd hours, once or twice a week, when it suits their convenience, will often work wonders. Instances of this may be seen in the fact that many colleges have of late years been materially assisted by a sturdy football player in the Torpid or Eight, and in the fact that Rugby football blues have rowed in the University Eight during the last three years. Another great difficulty which the captains of the smaller college boat clubs have to face is that of procuring good boats with very limited finances. The usual practice is to save up money for several years to buy a new eight, and to continue to row in her long after she has become practically useless, and, indeed, positively incompatible with good rowing. This is a difficulty which can to a great extent be got over by getting second-hand boats. These can be bought for about half price when they have only been used one or two seasons by the university, or by one of the larger (and therefore richer) college boat clubs, which can afford to get a new boat as often as they want one. By this means a college boat club, however poor, can always have a boat which, if not quite new, is at least comparatively modern, instead of being a water-logged hulk some eight or ten years old, such as one often sees wriggling along at the tail end of the Eights.

Yet another obstacle is there which it is not easy to overcome. It is often almost impossible to find a trustworthy coach. There is nearly always someone in residence who is considered capable of looking after the college Eight, but the ignorance of college coaches is often only too manifest from the arrant nonsense they may be heard shouting on the bank. There is only one remedy I can suggest. Let the college captain secure some member of the University Crew, or anyone else who knows what he is talking about, to take the crew for a couple of days, and make the College coach accompany him. He will thus learn something of the rowing of the crew, and you will hear him the next day pointing out the real faults to which his attention has thus been called.

In conclusion, I must add that, keen though the rivalry between the various colleges always is, it is a rivalry which, by the encouragement it gives to rowing, confers good and good only upon the interests of the O.U.B.C., and never degenerates into a jealousy which might be prejudicial to the success of the University as a whole. The college captains elect as president of the O.U.B.C. the man whom they consider to be best fitted for the post, to whatever college he may belong, for they know that the president will select his crew absolutely impartially, will never think of unjustly preferring men who belong to his own college, but will always do his best to serve the interests of the university.

College Rowing
At Cambridge

The casual visitor would scarcely imagine that Cambridge resembled either Macedon or Monmouth in the possession of a river. He sees in The Backs what looks rather like a huge moat, designed to keep marauders from the Sacred College courts, and filled with discoloured water, destitute seemingly of all stream. This he knows cannot be the racing river. The innumerable bridges forbid the notion, although Ouida has, in one of her novels, sprinkled it with a mixture of racing Eights and water-lilies. He wanders on from college to college, and nowhere does he come across the slightest sign of the river of which he has heard so much. Indeed, a man may stroll on Midsummer Common within about a hundred yards of the boathouses without suspecting the existence of the Cam. I can well remember convoying to the river an enthusiastic freshman who had just joined his college boat club. At every step I was asked whether we were yet approaching the noble stream. I answered evasively, and with an air of mystery which befits a third-year man in the presence of freshmen. At length we turned on to the common, which is bounded by the Cam; on the further bank stand the boat-houses. There were crowds of men busy in the yards, there were coaches riding on the nearer bank, but of the river itself there was no indication. We were still about two hundred yards away when a Lady Margaret Eight passed, the heads of the crew in their scarlet caps being just visible above the riverbank as they swung backwards and forwards in their boat. I felt my freshman's grip tightening on my arm. Suddenly he stood stock still and rubbed his eyes. 'Good heavens!' he said in an awestruck voice, 'what on earth are those little red animals I see running up and down there? Funniest thing I ever saw.' I reassured him, and in a few moments more we arrived at the Cam, crossed it in a 'grind,' and solved the puzzle. Distance, therefore, can scarcely be said to lend enchantment to the view, since at anything over one hundred yards it withdraws the Cam altogether from our sight. It is not easy, indeed, to see where the attractions of the Cam come in. It has been called with perfect justice a ditch, a canal, and a sewer, but not even the wildest enthusiasm would have supposed it to be a running stream, or ventured at first sight to call it a river. Yet this slow and muddy thread of water has been for more than seventy years the scene of excitements and triumphs and glories without end. Upon its shallow stream future judges and bishops and Parliament-men – not to speak of the great host of minor celebrities and the vaster army of future obscurities – have sought exercise and relaxation; to its unsightly banks their memory still fondly turns wherever their lot may chance to be cast, and still some thousands of the flower of our youth find health and strength in driving the labouring Eights and Fours along its narrow reaches and round its winding corners. It may well excite the wonder of the uninitiated that, with so many natural disadvantages to contend against, the oarsmen of Cambridge should have been able during all these years to maintain so high a standard of oarsmanship. Time after time since the year when First Trinity secured the first race for the Grand Challenge have her college crews carried off the chief prizes at Henley against all competitors, until, in 1887, Trinity Hall swept the board by actually winning five out of the eight Henley races, other Cambridge men accounting for the remaining three. The record of Cambridge rowing is thus a very proud one; but those who know the Cambridge oarsman and his river will find no difficulty in accounting for it. The very disadvantages of the Cam all tend to imbue the man who rows upon it with a stern sense of duty, with the feeling that it is business and not pleasure, hard work and not a picnic that summon him every day of the term to the boat-houses and urge him on his way to Baitsbite. We are forced to do without the natural charms that make the Isis beautiful. We console ourselves by a strict devotion to the labour of the oar.

The man who first rowed upon the Cam was in all probability a lineal descendant of the daring spirit who first tasted an oyster. His name and fame have not been preserved, but I am entitled to assume that he flourished some time before 1826. In that year the records of Cambridge boat clubs begin. There is in the possession of the First Trinity Boat Club an old book, at one end of which are to be found the 'Laws of the Monarch Boat Club,' with a list of members from 1826 to 1828, while at the other end are inscribed lists of members of the Trinity Boat Club, minutes of its meetings, and brief descriptions of the races in which it was engaged from the year 1829 to 1834. The Monarch Boat

Club was by its laws limited to members of Trinity, and, I take it, that in 1828 the club had become sufficiently important to change its name definitely to that of Trinity Boat Club. At any rate, it must always have been considered the Trinity Club; for in the earliest chart of the Cambridge boat races – that, namely, of 1827 – in the captains' room of the First Trinity Boat-house, 'Trinity' stands head of the river, and no mention is made of a Monarch Club. These ancient laws form a somewhat Draconian code. They are twenty-five in number, and eight of them deal with fines or penalties to be inflicted upon a member who may 'absent himself from his appointed crew and not provide a substitute for his oar,' or who may 'not arrive at the boathouse within a quarter of an hour of the appointed time.' There were fines ('by no means to be remitted, except in the case of any member having an ægrotat, exeat, or absit, or having been prevented from attending by some laws of the college or University') for not appearing in the proper uniform, for 'giving orders or speaking on a racing day, or on any other day, after silence has been called' (exception being made in favour of the captain and steerer), and for neglecting to give notice of an intended absence. To the twelfth law a clause was subsequently added enacting 'that the treasurer be chastised twice a week for not keeping his books in proper order.'

From the minutes of the Trinity Boat Club I extract the following letter, dated Stangate, December, 1828, which shows that even at that early date the first and third persons carried on a civil war in the boat-builder's vocabulary: –

Rawlinson & Lyon's compliments to Mr. Greene wish to know if there is to be any alteration in the length of the set of oars they have to send down have been expecting to hear from the Club, therefore have not given orders for the oars to be finished should feel obliged by a line from you with the necessary instructions and be kind enough to inform us of the success which we trust you have met with in the New Boat.

We remain Sir

Your obt Servts

Rawlinson & Lyon.

In 1833 it is curious to read, 'towards the end of this Easter term six of the racing crew were ill of influenza, etc., when the boat was bumped by the Queens', which we bumped next race, but were bumped again by them, and next race owing to a bad start the Christ's boat bumped us immediately being nearly abreast of us at the bumping-post.' Was this the grippe, I wonder? In the Lent Term, 1834, it is stated, 'The second race we touched the Christ's after the pistol was fired the first stroke we pulled, and lost our place to the Second Trinity for making a foul bump.' By the way, in the oldest minute-book belonging to the University Boating Club, extending from 1828 to 1837, I find the Second Trinity boat occasionally entered on the list as 'Reading Trinity.' It continued to enjoy this bookish reputation up to 1876, when a debt which continued to increase while its list of members as constantly diminished, brought about its dissolution. Its members and its challenge cups were then taken over by First Trinity.

In an old book belonging to First Trinity is preserved a map of the racing river, which explains much that would be otherwise inexplicable in the various entries. In those days the races began in the short reach of water in which they now finish. A little below where Charon now plies his ferry were the Chesterton Locks, and in the reach above this starting posts seem to have been fixed for the various boats. When the starting pistol was fired the crews started rowing, but apparently no bump was allowed before the bumping post, fixed some little way above the first bend where the big horse-grind now works. Any bump before this was foul, and the boat so fouling appears to have been disqualified. This post once passed, the racing proper began and continued past Barnwell up to the Jesus Locks. It must be remembered that the Jesus Locks were not where they are now, but were built just where the Caius boathouse now stands, there being a lock cut in the present bed of the river, and the main stream running quite a hundred yards south of its present course, and forming an island, on which stood Fort St George. This was altered in 1837, when the Cam was diverted to its present course, and the old course from above Jesus Green Sluice to Fort St George was filled up.

A few more extracts relating to the first beginnings of college boat-races may be of interest. In 1827 there were six boats on the river – a ten-oar and an eight-oar from Trinity, an eight-oar from St John's, and six-oars from Jesus, Caius, and Trinity, Westminster. In 1829 this number had dwindled to four at the beginning of the races on 28 February; but in the seventh race, which took place on 21 March, seven crews competed, St John's finishing head of the river, a place they maintained in the following May. Usually from seven to nine races appear to have been rowed during one month of the term, certain days in each week having been previously fixed. Crews were often known by the name of their ship rather than by that of their college.

I find, for instance, a Privateer, which was made up, I think, of men from private schools, a Corsair from St John's, a Dolphin from Third Trinity (which was then, and is still, the Club of the Eton and Westminster men), Black Prince from First Trinity, and Queen Bess from the Second or 'Reading' Trinity. The following regulations, passed by the University Boat Club on 18 April 1831, will help to make the old system of boat-racing quite clear:—

1. That the distance between each post being twenty yards will allow eleven boats to start on the Chesterton side, the length of the ropes by which they are attached to the posts being ten yards.
2. That the remainder of the boats do start on the Barnwell side at similar distances, but with ropes fifteen yards in length.
3. That there also be a rope three yards long fixed to the head of the lock, which will be the station of the last boat, provided the number exceed twelve.

These arrangements allowed thirteen boats to start at once, and special provision was made for any number beyond that. Obedience to the properly constituted authorities seems from an early period to have characterized the rowing man. I find that in 1831 a race was arranged between the captains of racing crews and the rest of the University, to take place on Tuesday 29 November. On the 28th, however, there arrived 'a request from the Vice-Chancellor, backed by the tutors of the several colleges that we should refrain from racing on account of the cholera then prevailing in Sunderland. We accordingly gave up the match forthwith, and with it another which was to have been rowed the same day between the quondam Etonians and the private school men.' The secretary, however, adds this caustic comment, 'It is presumed that Dr Haviland, at whose instigation the Vice-Chancellor put a stop to the race, confounded the terms (and pronunciations?) 'rowing' and 'rowing,' and while he was anxious to stop any debauchery in the latter class of men, by a slight mistake was the means of preventing the healthy exercise of the former.'

The umpire for the college races seems never to have been properly appreciated. Indeed, in 1834, the U.B.C. solemnly resolved 'that the umpire was no use ... and accordingly that Bowtell should be cashiered. In consequence of this resolution, it was proposed and carried that the same person who had the management of the posts, lines, and starting the boats should also place the flags on the bumping-post, and receive for his pay 4s a week, with an addition of 2s 6d at the end of the quarter in case the starting be well managed, but that each time the pistol misses fire 1s should be deducted from his weekly pay.'

In 1835, in consequence of the removal of the Chesterton Lock, the U.B.C. transferred the starting-posts to the reach between Baitsbite and First Post Corner, and there they have remained ever since.

Side by side with the college boat clubs, formed by the combination of their members for strictly imperial matters, regulating and controlling the intercollegiate races, but never interfering with the internal arrangements and the individual liberty of the college clubs, the University Boat Club grew up. With two short but historical extracts from its early proceedings, I will conclude this cursory investigation into the records of the musty past. On 20 February 1829, at a meeting of the U.B.C. Committee, held in Mr Gisborne's rooms, it was resolved inter alia 'That Mr Snow, St John's, be requested to write immediately to Mr Staniforth, Christ Church, Oxford, proposing to make up a University match;' and on 12 March, on the receipt of a letter from Mr Staniforth, Christ Church, Oxford, a meeting of the U.B.C. was called at Mr. Harman's rooms, Caius College, when the following resolution was passed: – 'That Mr Stephen Davies (the Oxford boatbuilder) be requested to post the following challenge in some conspicuous part of his barge: "That the University of Cambridge hereby challenge the University of Oxford to row a match at or near London, each in an eight-oared boat, during the ensuing Easter vacation."'

Thus was brought about the first race between the two Universities. Mr Snow was appointed captain, and it was further decided that the University Boat Club should defray all expenses, and that the match be not made up for money. It is unnecessary for me to relate once again how the race was eventually rowed from Hambledon Lock to Henley Bridge, and how the Light Blues (who, by the way, were then the Pinks) suffered defeat by many lengths. The story has been too well and too often told before. Each crew contained a future bishop – the late Bishop of St Andrew's rowing No. 4 in the Oxford boat, while the late Bishop Selwyn, afterwards Bishop of New Zealand, and subsequently of Lichfield, occupied the important position of No. 7 for Cambridge. Of the remainder more than half were afterwards ordained.

So much, then, for the origins of College and University racing. Thenceforward the friendly rivalry flourished with only slight intermissions; gradually the race became an event. The great public became interested in it, cabmen and 'bus-drivers decorated their whips in honour of the crews, sightseers flocked to the riverbanks to catch a glimpse of them as they flashed past, and their prowess was celebrated by the press. It is not, however, too much to say that without the keen spirit of emulation which is fostered by the college races both at Oxford and Cambridge, the University Boat Race would cease to exist. Truly a light blue cap is to the oarsman a glorious prize, but there are many hundreds of ardent enthusiasts who have to content themselves with a place in the college boats in the Lent or the May Term. Want of form, or of weight, or of the necessary strength and stamina may hinder them from attaining to a place in the University Eight, but they should console themselves by reflecting that without their patient and earnest labours for the welfare of their several colleges it would be impossible to maintain a high standard of oarsmanship, or to form a representative University Eight. Let me, therefore, be for a page or two the apologist, nay, rather the panegyrist, of the college oarsman, with whom many of my happiest hours have been spent.

Before entering upon the serious business of life as a freshman at Cambridge, the youth who is subsequently to become an oar will in all probability have fired his imagination by reading of the historical prowess of past generations of university oars in races at Henley or at Putney. Goldie who turned the tide of defeat, the Closes, Rhodes, Gurdon, Hockin, Pitman the pluckiest of strokes, and Muttlebury the mighty heavyweight, are the heroes whom he worships, and to whose imitation he proposes to devote himself. A vision of a light blue coat and cap flits before his mind; he sees himself in fancy wresting a fiercely contested victory from the clutches of Oxford, and cheered and fêted by a countless throng of his admirers. With these ideas he becomes as a freshman a member of his college boat club, and adds his name to the 'tubbing list.' He purchases his rowing uniform, clothes himself in it in his rooms, and one fine afternoon in October finds himself one of a crowd of nervous novices in the yard of his college boathouse. One of the captains pounces on him, selects a co-victim for him, and orders him into a gig-pair, or, to speak more correctly, 'a tub.' With the first stroke the beautiful azure vision vanishes, leaving only a sense of misery behind. He imagined he could row as he walked, by the light of nature. He finds that all kinds of mysterious technicalities are required of him. He has to 'get hold of the beginning' to 'finish it out,' to take his oar 'out of the water clean' (an impossibility one would think on the dirty drain-fed Cam), to 'plant his feet against the stretcher,' to row his shoulders back, to keep his elbows close to his sides, to shoot away his hands, to swing from his hips, under no circumstances to bend his back or to leave go with his outside hand, and, above all, to keep his swing forward as steady as a rock – an instruction to which he conforms by not swinging at all. These are but a few points out of the many which are dinned into his ears by his energetic coach. A quarter of an hour concludes his lesson, and he leaves the river a much sadder, but not necessarily a wiser man. However, since he is young he is not daunted by all these unforeseen difficulties. He perseveres, and towards the end of his first term reaps a doubtful reward by being put into an Eight with seven other novices, to splash and roll and knock his knuckles about for an hour or so to his heart's content. Next term (the Lent Term) may find him a member of one of his college Lent boats. Then he begins to feel that pluck and ambition are not in vain, and soon afterwards for the first time he tastes the joys of training, which he will be surprised to find does not consist entirely of raw steaks and underdone chops. Common sense, in fact, has during the past fifteen years or so broken in upon the foolish regulations of the ancient system. Men who train are still compelled to keep early hours, to eat simple food at fixed times, to abjure tobacco, and to limit the quantity of liquid they absorb. But there is an immense variety in the dishes put before them; they are warned against gorging (at breakfast, indeed, men frequently touch no meat), and though they assemble together in the Backs before breakfast, and are ordered to clear their pipes by a short sharp burst of one hundred and fifty yards, they are not allowed to overtire themselves by the long runs which were at one time in fashion. Far away back in the dawn of University rowing training seems to have been far laxer, though discipline may have been stricter, than it is now. Mr J. M. Logan (the well-known Cambridge boatbuilder) wrote to me on this subject: 'I have heard my father say that the crews used to train on egg-flip which an old lady who then kept the Plough Inn by Ditton was very famous for making, and that crew which managed to drink most egg-flip was held to be most likely to make many bumps. I believe the ingredients were gin, beer, and beaten eggs, with nutmegs and spices added. I have heard my father say that the discipline of the crews was of an extraordinary character. For instance, the captain of the Lady Margaret Boat Club used to have a bugle, and after he had sounded it the crew would have to appear on the yard in high hats and dress suits with a black tie. The penalty for appearing in a tie of any other colour was one shilling. The trousers worn on these occasions were of white jean, and had to be washed every day under a penalty of one shilling. The wearing of perfectly clean things every day was an essential part of the preparation.'

All this, however, is a digression from the freshman whom we have seen safely through his tubbing troubles, and have selected for a Lent Boat. I return to him to follow him in a career of glory which will lead him from Lent Boat to May Boat, from that to his college Four, and so perhaps through the University Trial Eights to the final goal of all rowing ambition – the Cambridge Eight. He will have suffered many things for the sake of his beloved pursuit; he will have rowed many weary miles, have learnt the misery of aching limbs and blistered hands, perhaps he may have endured the last indignity of being bumped; he will have laboured under broiling suns, or with snowstorms and bitter winds beating against him; he will have voluntarily cut himself off from many pleasant indulgences. But, on the other hand, his triumphs will have been sweet; he will have trained himself to submit to discipline, to accept discomfort cheerfully, to keep a brave face in adverse circumstance; he will have developed to the full his strength and his powers of endurance, and will have learnt the necessity of unselfishness and patriotism. These are, after all, no mean results in a generation which is often accused of effeminate and debasing luxury.

A few words as to our scheme of boat races at Cambridge. Of the Lent races I have spoken. They are rowed at the end of February in heavy ships, i.e. fixed-seat ships built with five streaks from a keel. Thirty-one boats take part in them. Every college must be represented by at least one boat, though beyond that there is no restriction as to the number of boats from any particular college club. No man who has taken part in the previous May races is permitted to row. In fact, they are a preparatory school for the development of eight-oared rowing. Next term is given up to the May races, which are rowed in light ships, i.e. keel-less ships with sliding seats. No club can have more than three or less than one crew in these races. In this term the pair-oared races are also rowed, generally before the Eights. The Fours, both in light ships and, for the less ambitious colleges whose Eights may be in the second division, in clinker-built boats, take place at the end of October, and are followed by the Colquhoun, or University Sculls, and next by the University Trial Eights, two picked crews selected by the President of the University Boat Club from the likely men of every college club. The trial race always takes place near Ely, over the three miles of what is called the Adelaide course. Besides all these races, each college has its own races, confined to members of the college. But of course the glory of college racing culminates in the May term. Who shall calculate all the forethought, energy, self-denial, and patriotic labour, all the carefully organized skill and patient training which are devoted to the May races; for so they are still called, though they never take place now before June? Every man who rows in his college crew feels that to him personally the traditions and the honour of his college are committed. The meadow at Ditton is alive with a brilliant throng of visitors, the banks swarm with panting enthusiasts armed with every kind of noisy instrument, and all intent to spur the energies of their several Eights. One by one the crews, clothed in their blazers, with their straw hats on their heads, paddle down to the start, pausing at Ditton to exchange greetings with the visitors. In the Post Reach they turn, disembark for a few moments, and wander nervously up and down the bank. At last the first gun is fired, the oarsmen strip for the race. Their clothes are collected and borne along in front by perspiring boatmen, so as to be ready for them at the end of the race. The men step gingerly into their frail craft and await the next gun. Bang! Another minute. The boat is pushed out, the coxswain holding his chain; the crew come forward, every nerve strained for the start; the cry of the careful timekeepers is heard along the reach, the gun fires, and a universal roar proclaims the start of the sixteen crews. For four 'nights' the conflict rages, bringing triumph and victory to some, and pain and defeat to others; and at the end comes the glorious bump-supper, with its toasts, its songs, and its harmless, noisy rejoicings, on which the dons look with an indulgent eye, and in which they even sometimes take part for the honour of the college.

Happy are those who still dwell in Cambridge courts and follow the delightful labour of the oar! For the rest of us there can only be memories of the time when we toiled round the never-ending Grassy corner, spurted in the Plough, heard dimly the deafening cheers of the crowd at Ditton, and finally made our bump amid the confused roar of hundreds of voices, the booming of foghorns the screech of rattles, and the ringing of bells. What joy in afterlife can equal the intoxication of the moment when we stepped out upon the bank to receive the congratulations of our friends, while the unfurled flag proclaimed our victory to the world?

To such scenes the mind travels back through the vista of years with fond regret. For most of us our racing days are over, but we can still glory in the triumphs of our college or our university, and swear by the noblest of open-air sports.

Rowing At Eton College

By W. E. Crum

In most books that have been published on rowing matters, a chapter has been devoted to rowing at Eton. But these accounts have been mainly of a historical nature, and have not, I think, dealt sufficiently with the career of an Eton boy, from the time when he passes through the ordeal of the swimming examination up to the proud moment when he wears the light blue at Henley, representing his school in the Ladies' Plate.

Before any boy is allowed to go on the river at all, he is obliged to satisfy the authorities of his ability to reach the banks of the river safely if he should upset while boating. This swimming examination is held about once a week after bathing has commenced in the summer half at the two bathing-places, Cuckoo Weir and Athens, which are reserved for the use of the boys alone.

On the Acropolis, a mound raised some ten feet above the water for diving purposes, sit the two or three masters whose duty it is to conduct the 'passing.' On one side a punt is moored, from which the boys enter the water head first as best they can. They have to swim a distance of about twenty yards, round a pole, and return, showing that they can swim in good style, and can keep themselves afloat by 'treading water.'

When a boy has successfully passed this examination, he is at liberty to go on the river. As it is probably well on in the summer half before he has passed, and it is more than likely that he has never before handled an oar, we will suppose that he does not enter for the Lower Boy races that year, but has to learn by himself, with no coaches to help him, the rudiments of rowing and sculling on fixed seats. Always on the river, whenever he has an hour to spare from his school duties, the Lower Boy soon acquires that knowledge of 'watermanship' for which Etonian oarsmen are famous.

By the end of the summer half, he can sit his sculling boat in comparative safety, and has learnt, perhaps, at the cost of several fines, the rules of the river, which are considered sacred by all Eton boys.

The ensuing winter terms are devoted to football and fives, rowing not being allowed; and we may pass on to the next summer, when our Lower Boy will probably enter for both Lower Boy sculling and pulling (i.e. pairs). These two races are rowed in boats almost peculiar to Eton. That used for the Lower Boy pulling is called a 'perfection,' of which the design is due to the Revd S. A. Donaldson; it is an open, clinker-built, outrigged boat, which recalls the lines of the old Thames wherry. That used for the Lower Boy sculling is known as a 'whiff,' an open clinker boat with outriggers. On an average about a dozen competitors enter for these events, five or six boats being started together, the first and second in each heat rowing in the final. The course, which is about two miles long, begins opposite the Brocas, extending for a mile upstream, where the competitors turn round a ryepeck, and then down-stream to the finish, just above Windsor Bridge.

If fairly successful in his school examinations, the boy whose career we are considering will, after his second summer, have reached the fifth form, a position which entitles him to be tried for the boats. He probably does not succeed in obtaining the coveted colour at the first attempt; and it is, say, in his third summer, that he first comes under the eye of a coach.

For the last month of the summer half, as many as ten or a dozen eights are taken out by members of the Upper Boats every evening, and four crews are selected from these, put into training, and carefully coached, and after about a fortnight's practice race against each other from Sandbank down to the bridge, a distance of about three-quarters of a mile; the race is called 'Novice Eights,' and each crew is stroked by a member of the Lower Boats. Every boy who rows in this race may be sure that he will get into the boats on the following 1 March; and having reached this important point in an Eton wet-bob's career, I must endeavour to explain the meaning of the term 'The Boats,' which I have already frequently used.

The Boats are composed of one ten-oared, and nine eight-oared crews, presumably made up of the eighty-two best oarsmen in the school; the boats are subdivided into two classes, Upper and Lower Boats.

The Upper Boats comprise the ten-oared Monarch, and the two eights, Victory and Prince of Wales; the Lower Boats are more numerous, consisting of seven eights, which have characteristic names, such as Britannia, Dreadnought, Hibernia, and Defiance. Each of the Upper Boats has a distinctive colour just like any other school team, whereas all members of the Lower Boats wear the same cap.

At the head of the Eton wet-bob world there reigns supreme the Captain of the Boats, who is always regarded in the eyes of a small Eton boy as next in importance only to the Prince of Wales and the Archbishop of Canterbury. He is captain of the Monarch, and after him, in order of merit, come the captains of the other boats, who act as his lieutenants; these captains are practically appointed by the first captain of the previous year, and were probably all members of the Upper Boats in that year.

At the beginning of each summer term the Captain of the Boats calls a meeting of his other boat captains; he has by him a list of all those who were already members of the boats the year before, and he knows pretty correctly the form of every one of them; thus, with his lieutenants' help he can assign to each oarsman the boat in which he considers him worthy to row.

The first boat to be made up is the *Monarch*. Though nominally the first of the boats, the *Monarch* is actually composed of those who, from their place in the school, or from their prowess at other games, deserve some recognition; in fact, I may best designate the members of the 'ten,' as good worthy people, who have tried to row well and have not succeeded.

The next boat is the *Victory*, and here we find the pick of the previous year's Lower Boats. Though junior, and in order of precedence below all the captains of the various boats, these eight have just as much chance of rowing in the eight at Henley as any of the captains; for the younger oar, whose faults can easily be cured, is often preferred to his stronger senior, whose faults are fixed and difficult to eradicate.

Similar to the *Victory*, though of rather a lower standard, is the *Prince of Wales*, or 'Third Upper;' and this is composed of the remnants of the previous year's Lower Boats who are not quite good enough for the *Victory*. The great distinction in the present day between Upper and Lower Boats is that all those in the former may row in any boat on sliding seats, while to those in the latter only fixed seats are allowed.

Having completed his Upper Boats, the captain has now to fill the seats in the seven Lower Boats. A few of the refuse, one may almost call them, of the year before are still left; refuse, because it is rarely the case that a boy who is more than one year in Lower Boats develops into a really good oar. To these are generally assigned the best places in the Lower Boats, and after them come, in order of merit, as far as possible, all those who rowed in the previous summer in the 'Novice Eight' race.

Thus, just as the Victory is always better than the Monarch, so the Dreadnought, the second Lower Boat, is often better than the Britannia, which may be composed of old 'crocks.'

On 1 March and 4 June in each year the boats row in procession, in their order, each boat stroked by its captain, up to Surley Hall, where, on the 4 June, a supper is held. But I will leave a description of the 4 June till later, and will return to where I left our successful Etonian, who has just received his Lower Boat colours.

During his first summer half in the boats he is practically never out of training. As soon as he has rowed one race he must begin practice for the next. The first race of the season is 'Lower Eights.' Four crews are chosen from among members of the Lower Boats, are coached for three weeks by members of the Upper Boats, and then race for a mile and a half. After this follow 'Lower Fours,' in which, again, four crews take part, chosen from the best of those who have raced in Lower Eights. These two races are rowed in order that those in authority may see how their juniors can race, and also that the said juniors may profit by efficient coaching. No prizes are awarded; they simply row for the honour of winning. After these come Junior Sculling and Junior Pulling, two races again confined to the Lower Boats. They are rowed in light, keelless, outrigged boats, with fixed seats, no coxswain being carried by the pairs. And here, again, much watermanship is learned, for the Eton course is a difficult one to steer, and only those who steer well can have any chance of a win. As many as fifty entries are sometimes received for Junior Sculling, for though an Eton boy may have no chance of winning a race, he will start, just for the sport of racing and improving his rowing, a proceeding which might well be imitated at Oxford or Cambridge. Each boy who starts in one of these races has to wear a jersey trimmed with a distinctive colour, and carry a flag in his bows; and it is extraordinary what ugly combinations some of them choose and think beautiful.

These four races have taken our young friend well on into the summer half; but after Henley is over, he will probably have to represent his House in the House Four race. Perhaps at his tutor's there may be one or two who have rowed at Henley in the Eight, and with these, and possibly another boy in Lower Boats, he has to train for another three weeks to row in what has been called, in a song familiar to Etonians of late years, 'the race of the year.' It is an inspiriting sight for anyone who wishes to get an idea of an Eton race to see the crowds of men and boys, masters and pupils, wet-bobs and dry-bobs, running along the bank with the race, some so far ahead that they can see nothing, some with the boats, some tired out and lagging behind, but all shouting for a particular crew or individual as if their lives depended on it.

In the last few years another race has been established for the Lower Boats; but it has not met with the approval of many Old Etonians. It is a bumping race, similar to those at Oxford and Cambridge, rowed by the different Lower Boats – Britannia, Dreadnought, etc. It is claimed that by practising for this race many of those who would not otherwise get much teaching are coached by competent people, and thus the standard of rowing is raised; but the opponents of the measure object, and as I think rightly, on the grounds that the average oar in the Lower Boats has quite enough rowing and racing as it is, and that even if more racing were needed, a bumping race is the very worst that can be rowed. It is necessary at the universities, on account of the narrowness of the rivers, to hold these races, for two boats cannot race abreast; but they must tend to make crews rush and hurry for two or three minutes, and then try to get home as best they can.

So much for the Lower Boat races. And there is only one more point to add concerning the Lower Boats: at the end of each summer half a list is published called 'Lower Boat Choices,' comprising about twenty of the Lower Boat oarsmen; to these also is given a special colour; and it is in the order of these choices that places in the Upper Boats are assigned in the following spring.

Having, therefore, in the next year, risen to the dignity of the Upper Boats, our Etonian has before him almost as many races as when he was in Lower Boats. His first is 'Trial Eights.' This takes place at the end of the Lent term, between two eight-oared crews, rowing on sliding seats, and chosen by the Captain of the Boats. It is from these two crews, picked from the Upper Boats and the boat captains, that the Henley Eight has to be chosen; and it is, therefore, the object of the first and second captains of the boats to equalize them as far as possible, so that they may have a close race, and that the rowing and stamina of individuals at high pressure may be watched. In the summer half come the School Pulling and Sculling, similar to junior races, but rowed on sliding seats, and confined to the Upper Boats. The winner of a school race, besides getting his prize, is entitled to wear a 'School Shield' – a small gold shield, on which are engraved the Eton arms, and the name and year of the race won. To secure a 'School Shield' is one of the greatest ambitions of every ambitious Etonian.

These two races being over, practice for the Eight which is to row at Henley begins. Every day the Captain of the Boats, aided by one or two masters, who have probably represented their universities at Putney in their day, has out two crews, composed of the best of those who are in Upper Boats. These crews are gradually weeded out till, perhaps, only an eight and a four are left; and then, at last, the Eight is finally chosen.

It is difficult to say who should be pitied most while this process of choosing the crew is going on – the captain or those who are striving for their seats; the captain always worried and anxious that he should get the best crew to represent his school, the crew always in agony lest they should be turned out, and should never be able to wear the light blue. Of course, the captain has the advice of those much more experienced than himself; but if there is a close point to settle, it is on him alone that the responsibility of the choice falls.

Once safely settled in the boat, there follows a period of five or six weeks of mixed pleasure and pain, for every crew, however good, must pass through periods of demoralization when for a few days they cease to improve, and periods of joy when they realize that, after all, they have some chance of turning out well.

For the last three weeks of this Henley practice the Eight is in strict training; but training for Eton boys is no great hardship. The days of 'hard steak and a harder hen' are over. The Eton boy is always fit, and the chief point he has to observe is regularity.

His meals are much the same as usual – breakfast at eight, lunch at two, a light tea at five, supper together at eight in the evening, and bed at ten. There is no need to pull him out of bed in the morning, as at the universities, for he has to go to school every morning at seven o'clock; he does not usually smoke – or, at any rate, is not supposed to by the rules of the school, and it is rarely that this rule is broken – and he does not indulge in large unwholesome dinners, after the manner of many undergraduates.

Every evening at six o'clock he goes down to the river, and is probably tubbed in a gig-pair before rowing down the Datchet reach in the Eight. About twice a week the crew rows a full racing course, and is taken in for the last three minutes by a scratch crew, which goes by the name of 'duffers,' composed of five or six Old Etonians and masters, and one or two Eton boys, who are kept in training as spare men. The crew is coached from a horse by one of the masters – of late years Mr de Havilland, who is certainly as keen for his crew to win as any boy in the school.

For the last five years the crew has taken a house at Henley for the days of the regatta, and gone to Henley by train the afternoon before the races. Though much wiser, this departure from Eton is not as impressive as in older days, when the crew used to drive to Henley for each day's racing; when, filled with pride and shyness, the young oarsman used to issue from his tutor's, wearing for the first time his light-blue coat and white cap, and walk to Mr Donaldson's or Dr Warre's house, where waited the brake which was to convey the crew, with the cheers of the crowd, along the hot, dusty road to Henley. In 1891, the last year that this drive was taken, the crew, before the final of the Ladies' Plate, had to drive no less than seventy-five miles in three days. They were only beaten by a few feet, and there is little doubt that but for this most tiring drive they would have won. Once at Henley, all is pleasure. No crew is more popular, none more cheered, as it paddles down the course to the starting point and as it arrives first at the winning post. The scene of enthusiasm, not only among Etonians, but among the whole rowing world, when an Eton crew wins the Ladies' Plate after a lapse of several years, is past description.

After Henley come House Fours; and then the list of Upper Boat choices is made up by the Captain of the Boats. The captain, by this means, appoints his successor for the following year, for he arranges these choices in order of merit, just as Lower Boat choices are arranged, and the highest choice remaining at Eton till the next year becomes captain. Thus the power of the captain is absolute; he can appoint whomever he likes to be his successor, and it is seldom that the choice falls on the wrong boy. Besides being the sole authority in these matters, the captain has to arrange all the money matters of the E.C.B.C.; over £500 pass through his hands in a year, and this gives an extra responsibility to his post. Of course all his accounts are carefully audited by one of the masters, and the experience gained, not only in looking after money, but also in arranging dates of races, in choosing and in captaining his crew, and in judging disputed points, is well worth all the trouble and worry entailed.

Our Eton Lower Boy has now reached the position of Captain of the Boats, and here I will leave him to go on either to Oxford or Cambridge and represent his university at Putney. A few words, however, may still be added.

There is a great difference between teaching a boy of sixteen and a man of twenty to row, and this difference lies in the fact that it is much easier, and perhaps even more important, to teach your boy to row in good form. By good form, I mean the power to use all his strength directly in making the boat move so that no energy is wasted in making the body pass through the extraordinary contortions and antics often seen in an inferior college crew.

It is easier to teach the boy of sixteen to row in good form, because his muscles are not yet formed, and his body still lithe and supple; it is more important to teach him, because he is not so strong as his elders, and consequently has not as much strength to waste.

A description of best how to use your strength would be out of place here, for it will be found set forth in another part of this volume. Let me, therefore, pass on to a subject which lately has caused considerable discussion – the subject of the length of the course for the Junior and School races. All these races are held over a course of about three miles in length, and take some twenty minutes to row. They start opposite the Brocas, and continue upstream round 'Rushes,' and then downstream to Windsor Bridge. The contention of many is that the length of these races is too great, and that the trial put on boys of perhaps fifteen years of age is too severe. From this view of the matter I differ, for to anyone who has rowed over both the Henley and Putney course it will be evident that the forty strokes per minute for a mile and a half would be more trying to a young boy than the thirty-four per minute for four miles.

A short note on the proceedings of the wet-bobs on the 4 June, the great day of celebration at Eton, may have some interest.

As I have said, a procession of all the boats takes place on this day. About five o'clock they start in order from the Brocas, and row to Surley Hall, where, in tents on the grass, a supper is prepared. After supping, they return to the rafts in time for a display of fireworks, the crews standing up in their boats and tossing their oars, whereby a very pretty effect is obtained. The dresses worn by the crews are quaint and old-fashioned on this great day. All are dressed in white ducks, a shirt of the colours of their boat, a dark-blue Eton jacket trimmed with gold or silver braid, and a straw hat covered with various emblems of their boat. The coxswains of the Upper Boats wear naval captain's clothes, while the Lower Boat coxswains represent midshipmen.

So much for Eton rowing; and, in finishing, I must pay a slight tribute to three old Etonians, to whom the success of

Eton rowing is mainly due. They are Dr Warre, the Revd S. A. Donaldson, and Mr de Havilland; and I feel sure that out of these three, who have all done yeomen service for their school, I may single out Dr Warre, and yet give no offence to his two successors. Before Dr Warre came to Eton as a master, in the early sixties, the masters had taken little interest in the proceedings on the river; consequently the traditions of rowing, learnt mainly from the riverside watermen, were not of a very high standard. Eton had never rowed in any races, except against Westminster, and it was due to Dr Warre's efforts that competition for the Ladies' Plate was first allowed. From this date till the middle of the eighties, Dr Warre was always ready to coach when asked, but never till asked, for he believed, and still believes strongly, in allowing the boys to manage their own games as far as possible.

How well he kept his principles of rowing up to date is shown in his pamphlets on rowing and coaching, for probably no one but he could have written so clear and concise a description as he has given.

Besides being an eminent coach, he understands thoroughly the theories of boat-building, his ideas being well exemplified of late by the boats which won for Eton in 1893, 1894, 1896, and 1897.

When the duties of headmaster became too engrossing to allow him to devote as much time to the Eight as formerly, his place was taken, and well filled, by Mr Donaldson. Mr Donaldson was always a most keen and patient coach, and followed closely on the headmaster's lines; and his cheery voice at Henley – clear above all the din of the race – once heard, could never be forgotten. He was very successful with his crews, and helped them to win the Ladies' Plate several times.

In 1893 Mr de Havilland first coached the Eight, and, since this date, has had an unbroken series of wins. In the first year of his coaching, fifteen-inch slides, instead of ten-inch, were used, and this, aided by his excellent advice, helped to produce one of the fastest Eights that Eton has ever sent to represent the school. Mr de Havilland has that wonderful knack, possessed by some good coaches, of training his crew to the hour, and it is surprising with what speed his crews always improve in the last week or so of practice.

I can only hope, in conclusion, that I have to some extent succeeded in explaining to the uninitiated the mysteries of the career of an Eton wet-bob during the five or six happiest years of his life spent at the best of schools.

Australian Rowing

By E. G. Blackmore

A country which has produced such scullers as Beach and Searle, not to mention Trickett, Laycock, Kemp, Nielson, Stanbury, and many others of less calibre, may well claim a place in a work treating of the science and art of rowing. In the limits of a chapter it is scarcely possible to give an exhaustive account of Australian oarsmen and oarsmanship, and as the performances of the leading Colonial scullers are sufficiently well known, from their having competed on English waters, this record will be almost entirely confined to amateur rowing, as practised in Australia.

That large continent, with the island of Tasmania, consists of six colonies, in all of which the art is cultivated, with more or less enthusiasm.

The first record we can find of anything like boat racing occurs in 1818, when ships' gig races were rowed in the Sydney Harbour, while the first regatta was held in the same place in 1827. In 1832 an Australian-born crew, in a locally built whaleboat, beat several crews of whaling ships. Passing over a series of years, in which nothing of more than local and momentary interest occurred, we find that in 1858, in the first race rowed on the present Champion course, the Parramatta River, Green beat an English sculler, Candlish, in a match for £400. I am inclined to regard this as the real foundation of New South Wales professional sculling, which afterwards culminated in the performances of Beach and Searle. The mother colony is the only one of the group which has produced a professional sculler of any class. Among amateurs none has yet appeared who could be placed in the first rank.

In all the Colonies there are rowing associations which regulate and control amateur rowing. Of these, New South Wales alone has attempted to maintain the amateur status on English lines. The other associations recognize men who would not pass muster at any regatta in the United Kingdom where the regulation definition obtains. To the New South Wales Association about ten clubs are affiliated. Under its auspices regattas are held in the harbour of Sydney, and one on the Parramatta River. The former water is utterly unfit for first-class racing, as it is exceedingly rough, exposed to sudden winds, and hampered with steam traffic of all sorts. In September – regarded as the commencement of the rowing season – there is an eight-oar race, the winners of which rank as champions for the ensuing year, and fly the 'Premiership Pennant.' On 26 January is held the Anniversary Regatta, which, founded in 1834, has been an annual event since 1837.

The Parramatta River course, on which champion events are decided, and which Hanlan, Beach, and Searle have made classic ground, is 3 miles 330 yards. It is practically straight, with a strong tide, the set of which is very difficult to learn. At times it is so affected by wind, as to render rowing impossible. The most perfect water is that of the Nepean River. Here a straight 3¼ miles course can be found, perfectly calm, and with no current. It was on this river that Beach beat Hanlan in 1887.

The Victorian Rowing Association holds three Championship events in the year – sculls, fours, and eights rowed in best boats on the Lower Yarra, and an annual regatta on the Albert Park Lake, though in former years it has taken place on the Upper and the Lower River. Important meetings are also held at Ballarat, Geelong, Warrnambool, Bairnsdale, Colac, Nagambie, and Lake Moodemere. The length for Intercolonial and Championship races is 3 miles 110 yards, with the tide, which may be set at three miles an hour.

The South Australian Association holds an annual regatta on the river Torrens, and has champion races for eights, fours, and sculls, on the Port River. The city course is one mile that for the champion races, three miles. The Torrens is at the best an inferior river for rowing, while the Port Water is a broad tidal stream, exposed to south-west winds, and at times exceedingly rough.

Queensland, Tasmania, and Western Australia, like their sister Colonies, have associations, and hold regattas.

The great event of the year is the Intercolonial eight-oar race, rowed alternately in Sydney, Melbourne, and Brisbane. Western Australia is now (1897) entering the field, but her crew is composed almost entirely of former Victorian oarsmen. In the past the rowing of Victorian crews has been generally far superior to that of the other Colonies, and in 1894 the Victorian combination was the nearest approach to English form that has yet been attained. South Australia has not so far been represented. Speaking generally, none of the picked eights of the Colonies have ever shown form or pace within measurable distance of the best college crews at Oxford and Cambridge, or the eights which may be seen at Henley. There is no approach to that systematic rudimentary teaching, coaching, and training, which proves so successful on English waters, and without which no crew can ever become that perfect human machine which a finished eight should be.

PUBLIC SCHOOL ROWING

Sydney

The principal rowing schools in New South Wales are the Church of England Grammar School, North Shore, the Sydney Grammar School, and St Ignatius College. Under the 'Athletic Association of the Great Public Schools' an annual regatta is held on the Parramatta River in May. The events are – 'Schools Championship,' Maiden Fours, Junior Eights, and a June Handicap Sculling Race. The association has fixed the distance at 1¼ miles. The races are rowed in string test gigs; and 8 minutes 15 seconds is considered good time for school crews, whose age, it must be remembered, does not equal that of English schoolboys. The boathouses of the two grammar schools are at Berry's and Woolloomooloo Bays, in the harbour; and they are at a disadvantage compared with St Ignatius College, which, at Lane Cove River, has a splendid course and smooth water. The ten days of the Easter vacation are spent by the two former schools in 'Rowing Camp,' i.e. they migrate to the Parramatta River, where there are better opportunities of systematic work and coaching. Each club, notably St Ignatius, has a good set of boats, those of the North Shore School being fitted with convertible fixed or sliding seats, carried on frames. The form of the two grammar schools is decidedly good, and conforms to the English standard much more nearly than that of most of the clubs.

Victoria

There are five schools approaching, as nearly as circumstances allow, the great public schools of England, viz. in the capital, the Church of England Grammar School, the Scotch College, Wesley College, St Patrick's College, and the Church of England Grammar School at Geelong.

Two races are rowed annually, for first and second crews, each school in turn having the choice of course, which is either on the Upper or Lower Yarra, the Albert Park Lagoon, or the Barwon at Geelong. For first crews the distance is 1¼ miles, for second a mile, the boats being string test gigs, fixed seats. Of all the schools none has a record equal to that of Geelong, where rowing, in comparison with other sports, occupies the same position as at Eton. To the Cambridge Eight it has contributed four oars, including the well-known heavyweight S. Fairbairn; while in the memorable race of 1886, when Pitman made his victorious rush on the post, the school had an 'old boy' in each boat – Fairbairn rowing for the Light Blues, and Robertson, whose father had been in Hoare's famous 1861 crew, for Oxford. In the Cambridge Trial Eights seven 'old Geelongs' have rowed; in the Oxford Trials only one; while the school has also been represented in the Grand Challenge and other races at Henley.

The Public Schools' Race for first crews was established in 1868, and for second in 1878. Geelong first rowed for the former in 1875, since when it has twelve wins to its credit, and the same number in the minor event.

The Boat Club was established in 1874, and at the present date has a roll of fifty-six members, an excellent boathouse, and nineteen boats. It holds an annual school regatta in June.

Rowing at the other schools is very spasmodic, mostly confined to a few weeks' training for the above races.

South Australia

There are only two schools in South Australia which merit the designation of public schools in the English sense, viz. St Peter's Collegiate School and Prince Alfred College, both in the immediate neighbourhood of the city.

Adelaide is bisected by the river Torrens, where, by reason of a dam, a mile and a half of water is available for rowing. But the course is so tortuous that racing is limited to a mile. The accumulation of silt is so great, and the growth of weeds and rushes so rapid, that for some five months in the year the river is kept empty for necessary operations; and at the best of times the water is slow and sluggish. At the annual regatta, under the Rowing Association, the rivals have often competed in a special race; but they ran the chance of being drawn to row private schools. In order to make rowing as important a part of school athletics as cricket and football, the present writer, who was then chairman of the Rowing Association, instituted in 1893 an annual race between these schools for a challenge shield, to be rowed on the tidal river at the Port, over a straight mile course. The boats used are half-outrigged, clinker, keelless fours and fixed seats, with a twenty-six-inch beam. The crews practise on the home water, and finish their preparation on the scene of the contest. So far, St Peter's College has won each event in the easiest style. A race has also been established with the Geelong school. Of three, each of which has been of the closest, Geelong has won once, St Peter's twice. The boats used are full outrigged clinkers, with sliding seats.

In spite of the inferior water, rowing at St Peter's is becoming almost as popular with the boys as cricket and football. To this state of things their success against Prince Alfred and Geelong crews has materially contributed, as well as the institution of school regattas. The club has a good boathouse, with the right class of boats for teaching and coaching, viz. steady, roomy, and half-outrigged, clinker fours, with keels, convertible as fixed or sliders.

UNIVERSITY ROWING

There are three Universities of Australia – those of Sydney, Melbourne, and Adelaide. Racing was first instituted when Sydney and Melbourne met on the water of the latter in string test gig fours over a three and a half miles course. In the following year they met on the Parramatta. Melbourne won on both occasions. The race was then discontinued, but in 1885 the Sydney University Boat Club was founded, and in 1888 the three universities mutually agreed to establish the race as an annual event in eights, to be rowed in turn on the Parramatta, the Yarra, and the Port Adelaide rivers, over a three mile course. Of nine races rowed – in two of which Adelaide, and in one of which Sydney, did not compete – Sydney has won four times, Melbourne thrice, and Adelaide on two occasions. The presentation by Old Blues of Oxford and Cambridge of a magnificent cup, to be held by the winners, has given a great stimulus to the race, and invested it with an importance which otherwise would not have attached to it. It has served to establish the continuity of the contest, and to connect the local Universities with their more famous elder sisters of England.

The Sydney U.B.C. undoubtedly takes the lead in prosecuting rowing. It promotes annual races for freshmen, and intercollegiate fours between the three colleges of St John's, St Andrew's, and St Paul's. Since their inauguration, in 1892, St Paul's has won on every occasion except in 1894. In 1895 and 1896 the U.B.C. won the Rowing Association Eight-Oar Championship.

There is an annual race in eights between Ormond and Trinity Colleges of the Melbourne University, besides a few other less important events, but the rowing spirit is not in such evidence as in Sydney and Adelaide. The latter is simply a teaching and examining university, with members so few that it is rather a matter of finding eight men to put in a boat than of picking or selecting a crew from a number of aspirants. Its success and enterprise are the more remarkable.

Speaking generally of university form in Australia, it is far inferior to that of a good college eight. Nor is the reason far to seek. There is no such recruiting ground as, for instance, Eton or Radley, not to mention other rowing schools, nor are there the opportunities for making oars such as the college clubs at the two great universities present, with the successive stages of the Torpids and Lent races, the May and Summer Eights, Henley, and the Trial Eights. Coaching, as in England, from the tow path or a fast steam launch, is practically impossible, and the number of those who have a scientific knowledge of oarsmanship, and, what is rarer still, the gift of imparting it to a crew, individually and collectively, is small indeed. Coaching in Australia is done from the stern, or from another boat, or by an occasional view from the bank, sometimes from a launch seldom fast enough to keep up, or range abeam. Pair-oar tubbing is of course utilized. Sydney University rowing is, however, far superior to non-university oarsmanship. The men sit up, use their backs and legs well, understand the knee work at the end of the slide, and do not rush their recovery. They are somewhat deficient in fore and aft swing, have a tendency to sky the feather, and rarely catch their water at the first. Melbourne rowing is wanting in body work, and conspicuous for absence of length. The men apparently are taught to discard on slides every approach to fixed-seat form, instead of to retain as much as possible. Thanks to a strong Oxford inspiration in Adelaide, and a belief in fixed-seat form as the foundation of good rowing on slides, an Adelaide school or university crew is conspicuous for length, reach, and swing. The pace of the eights is far behind English standard.

BOATBUILDING IN AUSTRALIA

It was the opinion of Hanlan that in the matter of boats and sculls he had never been so well served as by Donnelly and Sullivan of Sydney, a judgment as regards sculls endorsed by Beach and Searle. Chris. Nielsen, the sculler, has brought out a boat which he claims to be faster than the ordinary wager boat, with, against, or without tide, in rough water or smooth. The dimensions for an 11½ stone man are—length, 23 feet; beam, 16 inches; depth, 7 inches; forward, 6 inches; aft, 5½ inches; full lines throughout; height of seat from heel plates, 7 inches; height of work from seat, 5¾ inches; needs no fin, steers well, very light off hand; weight without fittings, 14 lbs. Riggers are bicycle tubing fittings, ordinary Davis gate; Colonial cedar, pine, and hickory timbers. The Australian-built boats are probably, so far as lines, general design, and workmanship, quite equal to the best English craft. For pairs, fours, and eights the Melbourne builders, Fuller, Edwards, and Greenland, are of the first class. They use a skeleton frame for the slides, built with angle pieces. This has all the rigidity of Clasper's more solid style, is lighter and stronger, and when the boat is being emptied allows the free escape of water. A Colonial eight is certainly lighter than those sent to Australia by Clasper or Rough. Probably the English builders have overestimated the weight of Australian eight-oar crews, which do not scale anything approaching a 'Varsity eight. Seating down the middle is generally preferred, which the present writer thinks has everything in its favour. The great drawback from which local builders suffer is the want of seasoned cedar. From this cause their boats do not last as long as English ones.

TIMES

I am not disposed to place much reliance on time as a test of a crew or a sculler, as conditions can never be so identical as to make comparison a safe guide. Still a certain interest attaches to records. It is contended that the Parramatta is a fifth slower than the Thames. The best trial with the tide that I know of is for a mile, 5 minutes 20 seconds with a four; 4 minutes 47 seconds with an eight. Over the whole course, 3 miles 330 yards, an eight has put up 17 minutes 12 seconds, one mile of which was compassed in 4 minutes 52 secs. On the Yarra the Victorian Eight of 1889 is said to have rowed two measured miles in 10 mins. 2 seconds At Brisbane, in 1895, the Sydney International Eight, with a strong stream, compassed three miles in 15 minutes, but the distance is doubted. On the Nepean course, 3 miles 440 yards, Sullivan beat Bubear in 19 minutes 15 seconds, no current.

Rowing In America

The sport of rowing, as I gather from Mr Caspar Whitney's well-known book was in its infancy in America when it had already taken a prominent place among our amateur athletic exercises in England. The Detroit Boat Club, established in 1839, was the first rowing organization in America. Next came Yale University, which established a Boat Club in 1843, and was followed by Harvard University in 1846. The first boat-race between Harvard and Yale took place in 1852 on Lake Winipiseogee, New Hampshire, in eight-oared boats with coxswains. Other meetings between these two followed at intervals until 1859, when a College Union Regatta was instituted. This took place at Worcester (Mass.), on Lake Quinsigamond, in six-oared boats without coxswains, the bow oar invariably steering, and was continued, with an interruption of three years during the Rebellion, until 1870, when the course was changed to the Connecticut River. Up to this time two universities only had competed besides Yale and Harvard; but in 1872 the number increased considerably, and in 1875 no less than twelve different Universities were represented in one race. These were, in the order in which they finished, Cornell, Columbia, Harvard, Dartmouth (Hanover, N.H.), Wesleyan (Middletown, Conn.), Yale, Amherst (Mass.), Brown (Providence, R.I.), Williams (Williamstown, Mass.), Bowdoin (Brunswick, Maine), Hamilton (Clinton, N.Y.), and Union (Schenectady, N.Y.). The most eventful of these big regattas was that of 1874 at Saratoga, when nine boats entered. Harvard and Yale, having adjoining stations, unfortunately became engaged in a dispute as to 'water,' and were left disputing by several boats. Harvard got away from the entanglement first, leaving Yale with her rudder and one oar broken, and went in pursuit of the others; but in spite of the most heroic efforts, were beaten by Columbia and Wesleyan, who finished respectively first and second. In 1876 Harvard and Yale decided to withdraw from these crowded meetings, and in this and the following year they rowed a private match at Springfield in Eights with coxswains, and in 1878 on the Thames at New London, where they continued their annual contest up to and including 1895. In that year there took place a break in the athletic relations between these two Universities, and in 1896 Harvard took part in a 'quadrangular' race with Cornell, Columbia, and Pennsylvania Universities. This was won by Cornell, Harvard being second, and was rowed on a perfectly straight four-mile course at Poughkeepsie on the River Hudson, where Cornell, Columbia, and Pennsylvania had decided some previous contests. In the present year, however, the differences between Harvard and Yale were happily adjusted, and a race was rowed at Poughkeepsie between them and Cornell, in which Cornell came in first, Yale defeating Harvard for second place. Harvard, Yale, Columbia, Pennsylvania, and Cornell possess at the present day the most important University rowing organizations, and at all of them the sport is practised with that intense keenness which characterizes the young American in everything that he undertakes. Especially is this the case with Harvard and Yale. Their rivalry has continued for many years, and a meeting between them in rowing, or in any other sport, evokes among their members an eagerness and an enthusiasm of which an Englishman can have little conception. Most of the universities that took part in the contests of the seventies seem to have dropped altogether out of the rowing world. Last year saw a new arrival in the shape of the University of Wisconsin. These Westerners, in spite of their difficulties of climate, were able to form a very good freshman crew, which defeated the Yale freshmen in a two-mile race. This year the Wisconsin University Eight rowed a two-mile race against the Yale University Eight, but were unable to make much of a show against them.

A Harvard Eight on the River Hudson at Ploughkeepsie.

The United States Naval Academy at Minneapolis can also put a very fair crew on the water, though the course of their studies allows them but little leisure for practice. This year they were defeated by Cornell in a two-mile race. The chief rowing school of America is undoubtedly St Paul's, at Concord, New Hampshire. It is divided into two boat clubs, the Halcyon and the Shattuck, and the teaching and training of the boys are looked after by Mr Dole, a man of great knowledge and experience in rowing matters. They practise on a large lake situated close to the school buildings, and show on the whole very fair form, though in this respect they cannot equal an Eton crew. Rowing recruits from this school are eagerly sought after by Harvard and Yale, in whose contests old St Paul's boys have a very brilliant record. At Groton School, in Massachusetts, the boys row in Fours on the river Nashua, their coach being Mr. Abbot, a graduate of Worcester College, Oxford. Rowing, however, at Groton has not yet assumed the importance it has at St Paul's, baseball being considered of the first importance, and the captain of baseball having the right to claim rowing boys for his team. Not a few Groton wet-bobs have, however, done well in Harvard and Yale crews. Besides these two rowing-schools, there is also the High School of Worcester (Mass.), whose Eight this year – the first, I believe, in its rowing history – rowed a severe but unsuccessful race against the Harvard freshmen on Lake Quinsigamond, and later in the summer won the race for Intermediate Eights at the National Regatta held on the River Schuylkill at Philadelphia.

To an English reader, with his experience of Henley Regatta, it will seem strange that the universities in America should take little or no part in any rowing contests except their own private matches, and should have no voice, and apparently no wish to have any voice, in the general management of the sport outside the universities. But such is the case. The National Association of Amateur Oarsmen of America has more than sixty clubs affiliated to it, but neither Harvard nor Yale nor Cornell is among the number. The National Association holds a successful regatta every year in August, but no really representative Eight from Harvard or Yale has ever, I believe, taken part in it. With that exception, this Association corresponds to our Amateur Rowing Association, and in its constitution states its object to be 'the advancement and improvement of rowing among amateurs.' By Article III. of the Association an amateur is defined as

> one who does not enter in an open competition; or for either
> a stake, public or admission money, or entrance fee; or

compete with or against a professional for any prize; who has never taught, pursued, or assisted in the pursuit of athletic exercises as a means of livelihood; whose membership of any rowing or other athletic club was not brought about, or does not continue, because of any mutual agreement or understanding, expressed or implied, whereby his becoming or continuing a member of such club would be of any pecuniary benefit to him whatever, direct or indirect; who has never been employed in any occupation involving any use of the oar or paddle; who rows for pleasure or recreation only, and during his leisure hours; who does not abandon or neglect his usual business or occupation for the purpose of training, and who shall otherwise conform to the rules and regulations of this Association (as adopted August 28, 1872, amended January 20, 1876, and July 18, 1888).

Any club which shall issue or accept a challenge for the purpose of holding a professional race, shall be for ever debarred from entering an individual or crew in the Regattas of the Association, and such club, if connected with the Association, shall be expelled.

In point of strictness, it will be noticed this Rule does not suffer by comparison with that of our own Amateur Rowing Association. Indeed, in some respects it is both fuller and stricter. Practically the only difference is that whereas we disqualify as an amateur one who has been employed in manual labour for money or wages, or who is or has been by trade or employment for wages a mechanic, artisan, or labourer, or engaged in any menial duty, this exclusion finds no place in the American Amateur definition. The Laws of Boat-racing adopted by the Association are practically the same as our own.

It may be interesting to contrast the organization and management of rowing at an American university with the systems that a long tradition has consecrated at Oxford and Cambridge. In our universities, in the first place, each particular sport is entirely independent of all others. Each has its own club, its own funds, derived from the subscriptions of its members, and each manages its own affairs and arranges its own contests, except occasionally in the matter of convenience of date, without any reference whatever to the others. A don is usually treasurer of these clubs, but he has no special authority or control merely because he is a don. His experience and greater knowledge are placed at the disposal of undergraduates in matters of finance; that is all. Certain general University rules as to time of residence, etc., have to be observed, but beyond this the dons assume absolutely no authority at all in the sports of the undergraduates. The undergraduates themselves, through undergraduate officers, elected by themselves, make all their own arrangements as to dates, matches, and everything else connected with their competitions; and a don would as soon think of flirting with a barmaid as of interfering with these matters in virtue of his donship. This point is really of capital importance. The responsibility of everything connected with the sports of the university thus falls upon the proper shoulders – those, namely, of the undergraduates who take part in them. The full glory of the victory is theirs, and a defeat they must feel is due to them alone. They cannot shift the blame to any don or committee of dons, and, as they must acknowledge themselves responsible, so the necessity of taking steps to restore the fortunes of their club is the more strongly brought home to them. The captain of a Boat Club is its absolute autocrat as regards work and discipline and the selection of his crew. The coach whom he asks to instruct them may possibly be old enough to be his father, but the coach, none the less, defers with an almost filial respect to the captain, through whom all executive orders are issued. In practice, of course, the wise captain is guided in most matters by his coach, but, should a serious difference arise between them, it is the coach who must give way to the authority of the captain. This uncontrolled management of their sports by the undergraduates is, it seems to me, no unimportant part of a university education; and a man may learn from it even more valuable lessons in conduct, self-control, and the treatment of his fellow men, than from all the books, papers, and examinations of his university curriculum.

At an American university a very different situation exists. I will take the case of Harvard, not merely because it is more familiar to me, but because it is typical in its general features, though not, of course, in all its details, of the position taken up by the authorities at most American universities with regard to the sports of the undergraduates. From the earliest days of athletic exercises the faculty, or governing body, of the university has kept a very tight control over them. It has issued rules and ordinances, allowing or forbidding certain competitions, deciding not only the number, but the date and place of matches in which it was allowable to take part, and regulating and controlling the conduct of those undergraduates who took part in athletics. This system, no doubt, originated at a time when the numbers at Harvard were comparatively small, and when the men entered College at an age considerably younger than is usual in England. But the numbers at Harvard have increased by leaps and bounds, and the age of undergraduates is now on an average the same as at Oxford and Cambridge.

In recent years, indeed, a slight change has been found advisable. The control of all athletics, whether rowing, baseball, football, or track athletics, is vested in what is called an Athletic Committee, composed of three professors (Anglicé, dons), three graduates of the university, and three undergraduates. These nine, who are not selected on any representative system, promulgate laws, conduct negotiations, settle dates, and generally perform those details of business which in England are left entirely to the undergraduates. For instance, the negotiations for a resumption of athletic relations with Yale University were on the Harvard side managed by and through the Athletic Committee. Moreover, the Athletic Committee has in its hands the appointment of coaches for the crew, and for the football, baseball, and athletic teams. The captain of a crew or a team is, to be sure, elected by the undergraduates themselves, the established system being that the crew should, before disbanding itself, elect the captain for the ensuing year. But no election of this kind is valid until it has been confirmed by the Athletic Committee. From the above account, in which I have confined myself to facts, and have not attempted to criticize, it will be seen how profound the differences between athletic organizations at English and American universities are.

But there are further differences which have nothing to do with the system of control and management. An English university is composed of many colleges, each entirely independent, so far as the management of its affairs are concerned. An English University Boat Club is organized on the same principle. It is made up of representatives of all the College Boat Clubs, and combines these autonomous institutions for what may be termed Imperial purposes. College rowing at Oxford and Cambridge foments a keen and healthy rivalry, and to no small extent helps to keep up the standard of university rowing. In America, on the contrary, the university is one, and apparently indivisible. There are no colleges, and, therefore, there is no aggregation of College Boat Clubs such as we have at home. The want of this element is, no doubt, a serious disadvantage to an American University Boat Club. The only element of rivalry comes from the competition of the four different classes (i.e. years, as we should call them – freshmen; second-year men, or 'sophomores;' third-year men, or 'juniors;' and fourth-year men, or 'seniors') against one another in an eight-oared race in the spring. Beyond this there has been hitherto no internal competition between members of the University Boat Club. Compare this single race with the long series of contests in which an English University oarsman takes part. He may begin in October with the Fours, row in the University Trial Eights in December, and in the university crew in the following March. Then come the College eight-oared races in May or June, followed by Henley Regatta in July, to say nothing of pair-oar races, and sculling races, and College Club races, or of the various Thames regattas, in which he may take part during what remains of the summer. He thus gains invaluable lessons, both in watermanship and in racing experience, which are not open to his American cousin.

For this absence of competitions in an American University Boat Club, the severe American winter, which closes the rivers from about the middle of December until early in March, is only partly responsible. During October and November the rivers are open; but up to the present very little advantage has been taken of these valuable months. At Harvard there has hitherto been no race or series of races for Fours or Pairs or Scullers, and freshmen, during their first term, have been exercised on a rowing machine, when they might, with infinitely greater profit, have gained instruction on the water.

Early in January, when the undergraduates have returned from their short Christmas vacation, a 'squad' for the university crew has generally been formed and sent to the 'training-table,' and the men composing it have been put into regular exercise, consisting of running varied by occasional skating, and of rowing practice every day in the tank. When the ice breaks up in March an Eight appears upon the water, and practises regularly from that time until towards the end of June, when its race against the rival university takes place. This long period of combined practice has many obvious drawbacks, which will at once strike an experienced oarsman. I believe better results might be obtained by allowing members of the university 'squad' to take part in the Class races, and then, after a period of rest, selecting the University crew.

Notwithstanding, however, all these disadvantages, rowing at American universities has reached a high standard – a result due to the extraordinary earnestness and enthusiasm of those who take part in it. The American University oarsman is in every respect as strong and as well-developed in physique as the average Englishman. All he lacks is the prolonged racing

Coaching on the River Hudson.

experience, which makes the Englishman so formidable and robust an opponent. There are men among the old oars of Harvard, Yale, and Cornell, who have made skilled rowing their special study, and whose knowledge of all points of the game is fully as great as that of our English oars. Yale, in particular, has, during the last ten years, been able to turn out some wonderfully fine and powerful crews; but the tendency among the American university oarsmen, during recent years, has been to sacrifice body swing to the mere piston action of the legs on a very long slide. There is now, however, a reaction, due to the visits paid by Cornell and Yale to Henley in 1895 and 1896, and the long body swing and general steadiness, which are marked features of English rowing, are now being very successfully cultivated in America.

At the five chief rowing universities – Harvard, Yale, Columbia, Pennsylvania, and Cornell – it is also customary to train a freshman crew every year, not merely for the local class races, but for competition against one another, the races taking place a few days before those in which the university crews compete. This year Yale defeated Harvard by something more than a length, Harvard being about three-quarters of a length ahead of Cornell. The race – a two-mile one – was very severe, and the crews, considering their material, showed, on the whole, better form than that displayed by the university crews. A week later the Cornell freshmen defeated those from Pennsylvania and Columbia over the same course. It is surprising to see what good results can be obtained from these freshmen crews. The men composing them have, for the most part, not rowed before coming to the university; they have had no graduated system of instruction on fixed seats. Up to March, all their rowing has been done on hydraulic machines in the gymnasium. They then launch a sliding-seat Eight and practise for the class races at the beginning of May. After that they are carefully taken in hand, and trained for their race in June against the other universities. It is from this freshman crew, and from the older hands, who may have been rowing in the class races, that the 'Varsity crew of the following year will be recruited.

The number of students at American Universities is thus stated in Mr Caspar Whitney's book: Harvard, 3,100; Yale, 2,400; Pennsylvania, 2,500; Columbia, 1,600; Cornell, 1,800; as against about 2,400 at Oxford, and 2,800 at Cambridge.

I ought to add that the use of swivel rowlocks is almost universal in America, and that all their Eights are built with the seats directly in a line in the centre of the boat. Boats of papier mâché have had a great vogue, their builder being Waters of Troy; but there is now a reaction in favour of cedar boats, as being stiffer and more durable. The Harvard and Yale boats this year were built by Davy of Cambridge (Mass.), and were beautiful specimens of the art. American boats, however, cost at least twice as much as English boats. T. Donoghue, of Newburgh, N.Y., makes most of the oars that are used in first-class racing. They are lighter by a full pound than our English oars, and are every bit as stiff. It is a real pleasure to row with them.

A Recent Controversy: Are Athletes Healthy? – Mr Sanow's Views On The Training Of Oarsmen

It would not be right, I think, to send forth a new book on rowing without referring to the controversy that has recently been carried on in the columns of the *St James' Gazette* under the general title of 'Are Athletes Healthy?' The discussion, which concerned itself mainly with oarsmen, is naturally of very deep interest, not only to them, but to the fathers and mothers who are anxious about the welfare of their energetic sons, and who, if the charges alleged against rowing can be proved, will, of course, do their best to dissuade their offspring from indulging in this pernicious exercise. I should have preferred to discuss the matter in the earlier chapters of this book, but the printing was already so far advanced as to render this course out of the question, and I am therefore compelled to deal with it somewhat out of its place in this final chapter.

It would be idle to deny that there was some reason for beginning this discussion. Within the past two years three magnificent young oarsmen, Mr H. B. Cotton, Mr T. H. E. Stretch, and Mr E. R. Balfour, have died; the first after an illness of six months' duration, the other two after being ill for less than a fortnight. They were all Oxford men, had rowed in victorious races both at Putney and at Henley, and two of them – Mr Cotton and Mr Balfour – had been actually rowing and racing till within a short time of the attack that proved fatal to them. Mr Stretch had not raced, except in scratch Eights at Putney, since the Henley Regatta of 1896, some ten months before he died.

It has been asserted that these three untimely deaths were due directly to the severe strain undergone both in preparation for racing and in the actual races in which these oarsmen took part, and that had they been content with unathletic lives they might have lived on for many years. Can that be proved? I admit that I do not wish to think the allegation capable of proof, for these three were my familiar friends. I had coached and trained them all; with two of them I had rowed in several races; I had spent innumerable happy days in their society, and the sorrow I feel in having lost them would be terribly increased if I were forced to believe that our favourite sport had had any part in hastening their end. In these cases I will confine myself to stating facts within my own knowledge, and will leave those who read my statement to say whether on a fair view of the matter the exercise of rowing can be held blameworthy.

I may begin by saying that it is the invariable rule at Oxford to send all men who may be required for the University Eight to undergo a preliminary medical examination. This examination is no perfunctory one. It is conducted by Mr H. P. Symonds, a gentleman of very wide experience, especially among undergraduates, and I have known several instances in which, owing to his report, an oarsman has had to withdraw temporarily from the river, and has lost his chance of wearing the coveted blue. There has never been any question about yielding to Mr Symonds's judgment. His verdict, if adverse, has always been accepted as final both by the oarsman concerned and by the president of the Boat Club. In all the three cases with which I am dealing, Mr Symonds passed his men as perfectly sound in heart and lungs and in every other organ.

I take the case of Mr Stretch first, in order to eliminate it conclusively. The cause of his death was appendicitis, followed by severe blood-poisoning. It is quite impossible to connect this painful and malignant illness with rowing or with any other exercise. The appendix vermiformis, which is the seat of the disease, is an unaccountable relic in the internal organization of human beings; it is liable to be affected mysteriously and suddenly in the young and the old, and the only effective remedy, I believe, is by means of an operation which removes it altogether. Mr Stretch had, as I said, not trained and raced for ten months, and up to the moment of his illness had been in the enjoyment of robust and almost exceptional health.

Mr Cotton, whose case I now proceed to consider, was an Eton boy, and had rowed a great deal during his school days, though he had not been included in the Eton crew at

Henley. He was a man of small stature, beautifully built and proportioned, well-framed, muscular, strong, and active. On coming to Oxford he continued his rowing, and being a good waterman and a man of remarkable endurance and courage, he was in his second year placed at bow of the university crew. Altogether he rowed in four victorious Oxford crews, he won the Grand Challenge Cup at Henley twice as bow of a Leander crew, he won the Stewards' Cup in a Magdalen College Four, rowed Head of the River three times, besides taking part in many other races more or less important. During his whole rowing career I knew him to be unwell only once, and that was in 1893, when he suffered from a sore throat at Putney. In 1895 he rowed bow of the Oxford Eight for the fourth time. The training of this crew was a very anxious one. Influenza was very prevalent, and one after another the Oxford men were affected by this illness. There were only two exceptions, and one of these was Mr Cotton, who was never sick or sorry for a single day during the whole period of practice. Shortly after the race he came to stay with me. He was then perfectly strong, perfectly healthy, and in wonderfully good spirits, and showed not the least sign of being stale or exhausted. He told me himself, on my congratulating him on having escaped the influenza, that he had never felt better or stronger in his life than he did at that time. On the Easter Monday he bicycled from Bourne End to Oxford and back (a distance of nearly seventy miles as he rode it), and, as he had had to battle against a strong cold wind on the return journey, he was very tired on his arrival. On the following morning, however, he appeared perfectly well. Towards the end of that week he complained of feeling 'very lackadaisical and having a bad headache,' but he attached no importance to these symptoms, and soon after went back to Oxford with a view to rowing in the Magdalen Eight. The tired feeling and the headache, however, continued, and eventually got so bad that he had to take to his bed with a high temperature and all the other symptoms of violent influenza. This illness, neglected at the outset, almost immediately settled on his lungs, both of which were congested with pneumonia. Owing, as Mr Symonds himself told me, to his good general condition and his great strength, he fought through this, but in the meantime signs of consumption had declared themselves, and of this he died at Davos Platz in the following October.

With regard to Mr Balfour, the facts are these: He was a man of Herculean build and strength. He played in the Oxford Rugby Union Football team for two years, 1894 and 1895. In 1896 and in this year he rowed in the University Eight, and last July he rowed at Henley in the Leander Eight, and won the pair-oared race with Mr Guy Nickalls. I can answer for it that during all his races he was absolutely fit and well. I saw him daily at Henley, and, though I knew him to be strong and healthy, I was surprised not merely by his improvement in style, but by the great vigour he displayed in rowing. On the morning after the Regatta I saw him for the last time. He was then in splendid health and spirits. On the 12 August he shot grouse; on the following day, in very cold wet weather, he went out fishing, and came home wet through, complaining of a chill. On the following day he took to his bed in a high fever, with both lungs congested. The illness next attacked his kidneys, and soon after his life was despaired of. However, he rallied in an extraordinary way until symptoms of blood-poisoning declared themselves, when he rapidly sank, and died on 27 August. Now, this illness was due either to an ordinary chill or to influenza, or, as I have since heard, primarily to blood-poisoning, caused by leaky and poisonous drains at a place where he had been staying before his shooting excursion. A subsequent examination of these drains revealed a very bad condition of affairs immediately underneath the room that Mr Balfour had occupied. In any case it does not appear – and the strong testimony of the doctors who attended him confirms me in this – that Mr Balfour's death was due to his rowing. But an objector may say, 'It is true that neither in Mr Cotton's nor in Mr Balfour's case can death be directly attributed to rowing; their exertions, however, so exhausted their strength, the soundness of their organs, and their powers of resistance to disease, that when they were attacked they became easy victims.' To this I oppose (1) the report of Mr H. P. Symonds, who examined both these oarsmen before they rowed in their University Eights; (2) my own observation of their health, condition, and spirits during practice, in their races, and afterwards when the races were over; and (3) the reports of the doctors who attended them during their last illnesses, and who declared (I speak at second hand with regard to Mr Balfour, at first hand with regard to Mr Cotton) that they were both, when struck down, in a surprising state of strength, due to the exercise in which they had taken part, and that in both cases their powers of resistance were far greater than are usually found. Do I go too far in asserting that any doctor in large practice could find in his own experience for each of these two cases at least twenty cases in which non-rowing and non-athletic men have been suddenly carried off by the same sort of illness? I am not concerned to prove that rowing confers an immunity from fatal illness: my point is that in the two cases

I have considered, and in all cases where it is pursued under proper conditions of training and medical advice, rowing does not in any way promote a condition favourable to disease.

I pass from these particular cases, the discussion of which has been painful to me, to the general question of health among the great mass of those who have been, or are, active rowing men. It may be remembered that some twenty-five years ago Dr J. H. Morgan, of Oxford, moved to his task by a controversy similar to that which has recently taken place, instituted a very careful inquiry into the health of those who had taken part in the University Boat Race from 1829 to 1869. Their number amounted, if I remember rightly, to 294, of whom 255 were alive at the date of the inquiry. Of these 115 were benefited by rowing, 162 were uninjured, and only in seventeen cases was any injury stated to have resulted. And it must be remembered that this inquiry covered a period during which far less care, as a general rule, was exercised both as to the selection and the training of men than is the case at the present day. I may add my own experience. Since I began to row, in 1874, I have rowed and raced with or against hundreds of men in college races and at regattas, and I have watched closely the rowing of very many others in university and in Henley crews. I have kept in touch with rowing men, both my contemporaries and my successors, and among them all I could not point to one (putting aside for the moment the three special cases I have just discussed) who has been injured by the exercise, or would state himself to have been injured. On the contrary, I can point to scores and scores of men who have been strengthened in limb and health – I say nothing here of any moral effect – by their early races and the training they had to undergo for them. I could at this moment pick a crew composed of men all more than thirty years old who are still, or have been till quite recently, in active rowing, and, though some of them are married men, I would back them to render a good account of themselves in Eight or Four or Pair against any selection of men that could be made. Nay more, in any other contests of strength or endurance I believe they would more than hold their own against younger athletes, and would overwhelm any similar number of non-athletes of the same or any other age. As contests I should select a hard day's shooting over dogs, cross-country riding, tug-of-war, boxing, long-distance rowing, or, in fact, any contest in which the special element of racing in light ships has no part. For such contests I could pick, not eight, but eighty men well over thirty years old, and if the limit were extended to twenty-four years of age I could secure an army. Is there anyone who doubts that my rowing men would knock the non-athletes into a cocked hat? For it must be remembered that the bulk of rowing men are not exclusively devoted to oarsmanship. A very large proportion of those that I have known have been good all-round sportsmen.

As to the general effect of rowing on strength and health I may perhaps be pardoned if I cite my own case, not because there is anything especially remarkable in it, but because it bears on some of the questions that have been raised, and I can speak about it with certainty. In early childhood I had a serious illness which considerably retarded my physical development. At school, however, I took my part in all sports, played three years in the Cricket XI and in the Football XV, and won several prizes at the athletic sports. I went to Cambridge in 1874, when I was three months short of nineteen, and immediately took to rowing. I was certainly not a particularly strong boy then, though I had a fair share of activity. I rowed persistently in Eights, Fours and Pairs, at first with labour and distress, but gradually, as time went on, with ease and pleasure, and I found that the oftener I rowed the greater became my powers of endurance. I ought to add that I never rowed in the University Race, but I have borne my share in thirty-six bumping races, as well as in numerous other races ranging in distance from three-quarters of a mile to three miles. I believe that the six consecutive races of a May Term call for endurance at least as great as the single race from Putney to Mortlake. My actual muscular strength, too, increased very largely, and has ever since maintained itself unimpaired. I have found that this exercise has, in fact, strengthened and consolidated me all round; and I can think of no other exercise that could have had upon me the same salutary effect that I am justified in attributing mainly to rowing – an effect which has enabled me to endure great exertion, sometimes in extremes of heat or of cold, without the smallest ill result, and has brought me to middle age with sound organs, a strong constitution, active limbs, and a good digestion. There are hundreds of other men who could, I doubt not, give a similar account of themselves.

Out of this main discussion on the health of athletes there sprang a subsidiary one, which proved of even greater interest to rowing men. It was started by Mr Sandow, the eminent weight-lifter and modern representative of Hercules. Mr Sandow, stimulated by a disinterested love for his fellow-men in general, and for those of Cambridge University in particular, wrote an article in the *St James's Gazette* in which he put forward his own peculiar views on the proper system for the training of athletes. He ended by declaring that if he were allowed to train a

Cambridge crew according to his system (it being understood that rowing instruction was at the same time to be imparted to them by a properly qualified teacher), he would guarantee to turn out a crew the like of which had never before sat in a boat. We were to infer, though this was at first sight not obvious, that this crew would easily defeat an Oxford crew trained on a system which Mr Sandow evidently considered to be absurd and obsolete.

According to Mr Sandow's system, as he subsequently developed it, the members of this crew were to have complete license in all things. They were to eat what they liked, drink what they liked, smoke as much as they liked, and, in fact, make their own good pleasure the supreme law of their existence. All that Mr Sandow stipulated was that for some two hours a day during a period of several months these men were to put themselves in Mr Sandow's hands for the purpose of muscular development all round according to the methods usually employed by him. Any spare energy that might then remain to them might be devoted to the work of rowing in the boat.

Now, in the first place, there are certain elementary difficulties which would go far to prevent the adoption of this experiment. The crew is not selected several months before the race; and even if it were, it would be practically impossible for the men composing it to spare the time required by Mr Sandow. After all, even the most brilliant of us have to get through a certain amount of work for our degrees. There are lectures to be attended, there is private reading, not to speak of the time which has to be devoted to the ordinary social amenities of life at a university. Sport has its proper place in the life of an undergraduate; but it does not, and cannot, absorb the whole of that life. Yet if a man is to spend two hours with Mr Sandow, and about two hours and a half (I calculate from the moment he leaves his rooms until he returns from the river) on the exercise of rowing, it is not easy to see how he will have sufficient vigour left to him to tackle the work required even for the easiest of pass examinations. I can foresee that not only the man himself, but his tutors and his parents might offer some rather serious objections.

But I am not going to content myself with pointing out these preliminary difficulties. I go further, and say that the whole proposal is based upon a fallacy. The method of training and development that may fit a man admirably for the purpose of weightlifting, or of excelling his fellow creatures in the measurement of his chest and his muscles, is utterly unsuited for a contest that requires great quickness of movement, highly developed lung power, and general endurance spread over a period of some twenty minutes. It does not follow that because a man measures forty-two inches round the chest, and has all his muscles developed in proportion, he will therefore be better fitted for the propulsion of a racing boat than a man who in all points of development is his inferior. If I produced Mr C. W. Kent incognito before Mr Sandow and asked whether it would be feasible to include this gentleman in an eight-oared crew, Mr Sandow would probably laugh me to scorn. Mr Sandow could doubtless hold out Mr Kent at arm's length with the greatest possible ease. I am perfectly certain that Mr Kent – if he will pardon me for thus making free with his name – could do nothing of the kind to Mr Sandow. Yet I am perfectly certain, too, that, in a severely contested race, Mr Kent – admittedly one of the finest strokes that ever rowed – would, to put it mildly, be more useful than Mr Sandow. All gymnasium work, and even the modified form of it patented by Mr Sandow, must tend to make men muscle-bound, and therefore slow. Skilled rowing consists of a series of movements which have to be gone through with a peculiar quickness, precision, and neatness. To be able to go through Mr Sandow's eight weight exercises, to lift weights, to carry horses on your chest, may indicate great muscular strength, but it has absolutely nothing to do with being able to row. If a rowing man requires some exercise subsidiary to rowing, he would, in my opinion, be far better advised if he devoted some of his spare time to boxing and to fencing, exercises which necessitate immense quickness and perfect combination between brain, hand, and eye, than if he were to spend time in building up his body with such exercises as are included in the Sandow curriculum. But, in the main, rowing must develop for itself the muscles it requires. It is an exercise which, when all is said and done, can only be learnt effectively in a boat on the water. It is thus, and thus only, that a man can acquire the necessary movements, and perfect himself in that sense of balance and of rhythm which is as necessary to a rowing man as muscular strength. My experience leads me to the conclusion that men who, though naturally well-framed and proportioned, are not afflicted with excessive muscle, are more likely to be useful in rowing than the pet of a gymnasium or the muscle-bound prodigies made in the image of Mr Sandow. I may cite as examples such men as Mr R. P. P. Rowe, Mr R. O. Kerrison, Mr W. Burton Stewart, Mr W. E. Crum, Mr J. A. Ford, and Mr C. W. Kent. All these men acquired their unquestionable excellence as oarsmen by the only possible method – that is, by long practice of rowing in boats. Even an exercise so nearly resembling actual rowing as the tank work practised in the winter by American crews has very serious disadvantages. It might be supposed that it would exercise and keep in trim the muscles required for actual rowing; but its effect is to make men slow and heavy, faults which they have to correct when they once more take to the river.

With regard to Mr Sandow's revolutionary proposals about diet, smoking, and hours, I have only this to say. We rowing men have shown time after time that by adhering to what I do not hesitate to call our common-sense system of rules tempered with indulgences we can bring our men to the post in the most perfect health and condition, absolutely fit, so far as their wind and powers of endurance are concerned, to take part in the severest contests. What has Mr Sandow shown that should avail, with these results before our eyes, to make us exchange our disciplined liberty for his unfettered license? In the mean time we shall very properly hesitate to take the leap in the dark that he suggests.

I trust that the President of the C.U.B.C. will, in future, conduct the practice of his crew according to the methods that have proved their efficacy over and over again, and that he will not listen to the voice of Mr Sandow, charm he never so unwisely. *Non tali auxilio* are boat-races to be won.

ROWING TYPES.
NO. 1.

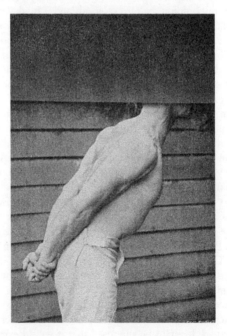

NO. 2.

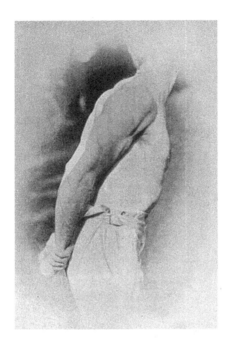

NO. 3.

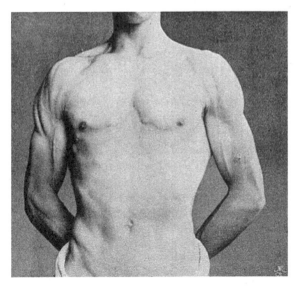

NO. 4.

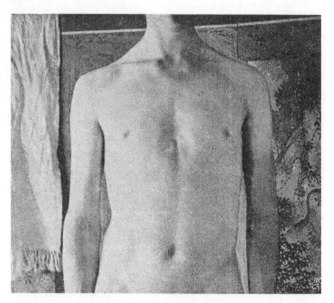

NO. 5.

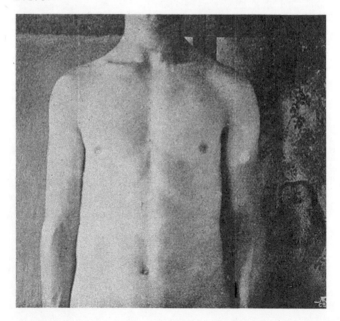

Appendix

HENLEY ROYAL REGATTA

Secretary: J. F. Cooper.

Qualification Rules

The Grand Challenge Cup, For Eight Oars.
Any crew of amateurs who are members of any University or public school, or who are officers of Her Majesty's army or navy, or any amateur club established at least one year previous to the day of entry, shall be qualified to contend for this prize.

The Stewards' Challenge Cup, For Four Oars.
The same as for the Grand Challenge Cup.

The Ladies' Challenge Plate, For Eight Oars.
Any crew of amateurs who are members of any of the boat clubs of colleges, or non-collegiate boat clubs of the Universities, or boat clubs of any of the public schools, in the United Kingdom only, shall be qualified to contend for this prize; but no member of any college or non-collegiate crew shall be allowed to row for it who has exceeded four years from the date of his first commencing residence at the University; and each member of a public school crew shall, at the time of entering, be bona fide a member 'in statu pupillari' of such school.

The Visitors' Challenge Cup, For Four Oars.
The same as for the Ladies' Challenge Plate.

The Thames Challenge Cup, For Eight Oars.
The qualification for this cup shall be the same as for the Grand Challenge Cup; but no one (coxswains excepted) may enter for this cup who has ever rowed in a winning crew for the

Grand Challenge Cup or Stewards' Challenge Cup; and no one (substitutes as per Rule II excepted) may enter, and no one shall row, for this cup and for the Grand Challenge Cup, or Stewards' Challenge Cup, at the same regatta.

The Wyfold Challenge Cup, For Four Oars.

The qualification for this cup shall be the same as for the Stewards' Challenge Cup; but no one shall enter for this cup who has ever rowed in a winning crew for the Stewards' Challenge Cup; and no one (substitutes as per Rule II excepted) may enter, and no one shall row, for this cap and for the Stewards' Challenge Cup at the same regatta.

The Silver Goblets, For Pair Oars.

Open to all amateurs duly entered for the same according to the Rules following.

The Diamond Challenge Sculls, For Sculls.

Open to all amateurs duly entered for the same according to the Rules following.

GENERAL RULES.

Revised 1 December 1894.

Definition.
I. No person shall be considered an amateur oarsman, sculler or coxswain

1. Who has ever rowed or steered in any race for a stake, money, or entrance-fee.
2. Who has ever knowingly rowed or steered with or against a professional for any prize.
3. Who has ever taught, pursued, or assisted in the practice of athletic exercises of any kind for profit.
4. Who has ever been employed in or about boats, or in manual labour, for money or wages.
5. Who is or has been by trade or employment for wages, a mechanic, artisan, or labourer, or engaged in any menial duty.
6. Who is disqualified as an amateur in any other branch of sport.

Eligibility.

II. No one shall be eligible to row or steer for a club unless he has been a member of that club for at least two months preceding the regatta, but this rule shall not apply to colleges, schools, or crews composed of officers of Her Majesty's army or navy.

Entries.

III. The entry of any amateur club, crew, or sculler, in the United Kingdom, must be made ten clear days before the regatta, and the names of the captain or secretary of each club or crew must accompany the entry. A copy of the list of entries shall be forwarded by the secretary of the regatta to the captain or secretary of each club or crew duly entered.

IV. The entry of any crew or sculler, out of the United Kingdom, other than a crew or sculler belonging to a club affiliated to the Union des Sociétés Françaises de Sports Athlétiques, or of the Deutscher Ruder Verband, or of the Verbonden Nederlandsche Roeivereenigingen, must be made on or before the 31 March, and any such entry must be accompanied by a declaration made before a notary public, with regard to the profession of each person so entering, to the effect that he has never rowed or steered in any race for a stake, money, or entrance fee; has never knowingly rowed or steered with or against a professional for any prize; has never taught, pursued, or assisted in the practice of athletic exercises of any kind for profit; has never been employed in or about boats, or in manual labour for money or wages; is not, and never has been, by trade or employment, for wages, a mechanic, artisan, or labourer, or engaged in any menial duty; and is not disqualified as an amateur in any other branch of sport; and in cases of the entry of a crew, that such crew represents a club which has been duly established at least one year previous to the day of entry: and such declaration must be certified by the British Consul or the mayor, or the chief authority of the locality.

The entry of any crew or sculler belonging to a club affiliated to the Union des Sociétés Françaises de Sports Athlétiques, or of the Deutscher Ruder Verband, or of the Verbonden Nederlandsche Roeivereenigingen, must be made on or before the 1 June, and any such entry must be accompanied by a declaration in writing by the secretary of such Union, or Verband, or by the Council of the club from time to time appointed by the Verbonden Nederlandsche Roeivereenigingen, with regard to the profession of each person so entering, to the effect that he has never since the institution of the Union des Sociétés Françaises de Sports Athlétiques, or the Deutscher Ruder Verband, or of the Verbonden Nederlandsche Roeivereenigingen, as the case may be, either rowed or steered in any race for a stake, money, or entrance fee; or knowingly rowed or steered with or against a professional for any prize; has never taught, pursued, or assisted in the practice of athletic exercises of any kind for profit; has never been employed in or about boats, or in manual labour for money or wages; is not, and never has been by trade or employment, for wages, a mechanic, artisan, or labourer, or engaged in any menial duty; and is not disqualified as an amateur in any other branch of sport; and in cases of the entry of a crew, that each member thereof is and has been for two months a member of such club, and that such club has been duly established at least one year previous to the day of entry.

V. No assumed name shall be given to the secretary unless accompanied by the real name of the competitor.

VI. No one shall enter twice for the same race.

VII. No official of the regatta shall divulge any entry, or report the state of the entrance list, until such list be closed.

VIII. Entrance money for each boat shall be paid to the secretary at the time of entering, as follows:—

For the Grand Challenge Cup £6 6s 0d
For the Ladies' Challenge Plate £5 5s 0d
For the Thames Challenge Cup £5 5s 0d
For the Stewards' Challenge Cup £4 4s 0d
For the Visitors' Challenge Cup £3 3s 0d
For the Wyfold Challenge Cup £3 3s 0d
For the Silver Goblets £2 2s 0d
For the Diamond Challenge Sculls £1 1s 0d

IX. The Committee shall investigate any questionable entry, irrespective of protest.

X. The Committee shall have power to refuse or return any entry up to the time of starting, without being bound to assign a reason.

XI. The captain or secretary of each club or crew entered shall, seven clear days before the regatta, deliver to the secretary of the regatta a list containing the names of the actual crew appointed to compete, to which list the names of not more than four other members for an eight-oar and two for a four-oar may be added as substitutes.

XII. No person may be substituted for another who has already rowed or steered in a heat.

XIII. The secretary of the regatta, after receiving the list of the crews entered, and of the substitutes, shall, if required, furnish a copy of the same, with the names, real and assumed, to the captain or secretary of each club or crew entered, and in the case of pairs or scullers to each competitor entered.

Objections.

XIV. Objections to the entry of any club or crew must be made in writing to the secretary at least four clear days before the regatta, when the committee shall investigate the grounds of objection, and decide thereon without delay.

XV. Objections to the qualification of a competitor must be made in writing to the secretary at the earliest moment practicable. No protest shall be entertained unless lodged before the prizes are distributed.

Course.

XVI. The races shall commence below the Island, and terminate at the upper end of Phyllis Court. Length of course, about 1 mile and 550 yards.

XVII. The whole course must be completed by a competitor before he can be held to have won a trial or final heat.

Stations.

XVIII. Stations shall be drawn by the Committee.

Row over.

XIX. In the event of there being but one boat, entered for any prize, or if more than one enter, and all withdraw but one, the crew of the remaining boat must row over the course to be entitled to such prize.

Heats.

XX. If there shall be more than two competitors, they shall row a trial heat or heats; but no more than two boats shall contend in any heat for any of the prizes above mentioned.

XXI. In the event of a dead heat taking place, the same crews shall contend again, after such interval as the Committee may appoint, or the crew refusing shall be adjudged to have lost the heat.

Clothing.

XXII. Every competitor must wear complete clothing from the shoulders to the knees—including a sleeved jersey.

Coxswains.

XXIII. Every eight-oared boat shall carry a coxswain; such coxswain must be an amateur, and shall not steer for more than one club for the same prize.

The minimum weight for coxswains shall be 7 stone.

Crews averaging 10½ stone and under 11 stone to carry not less than 7½ stone.

Crews averaging 11 stone or more, to carry not less than 8 stone.

Deficiencies must be made up by dead weight carried on the coxswain's thwart.

The dead weight shall be provided by the Committee, and shall be placed in the boat and removed from it by a person appointed for that purpose.

Each competitor (including the coxswain) in eight and four-oared races shall attend to be weighed (in rowing costume) at the time and place appointed by the Committee: and his weight then registered by the secretary shall be considered his racing weight during the regatta.

Any member of a crew omitting to register his weight shall be disqualified.

Flag.

XXIV. Every boat shall, at starting, carry a flag showing its colour at the bow. Boats not conforming to this Rule are liable to be disqualified at the discretion of the umpire.

Umpire.

XXV. The Committee shall appoint one or more umpires to act under the laws of boat-racing.

Judge.

XXVI. The Committee shall appoint one or more judges, whose decision as to the order in which the boats pass the post shall be final.

Prizes.

XXVII. The prizes shall be delivered at the conclusion of the regatta to the respective winners, who on receipt of a challenge prize shall subscribe a document of the following effect:—

I/We A (B C D, etc.) (members of the club), having been this day declared to be the winners of the Henley Royal Regatta Challenge Cup (or diamond sculls), and the same having been delivered to us on behalf of the stewards of the said regatta, do (jointly and severally) agree to return in good order and condition as now received the said cup (or diamond sculls), to the stewards on or before June 1st next, and I/we do also (jointly and severally) agree that if the said cup (or sculls) be accidentally lost or destroyed, or in any way permanently defaced, I/we will on or before the date aforesaid, or as near thereto as may be conveniently possible, place in the hands of the said stewards a cup (or diamond sculls) of similar design and value, and engraved with the names of the previous winners (their officers) (and crews) as now engraved on the present cup and base./case. In witness of which agreement I/we have hereunto subscribed my/our (respective) name./names.

Committee.

XXVIII. All questions of eligibility, qualification, interpretation of the Rules, or other matters not specially provided for, shall be referred to the Committee, whose decision shall be final.

XXIX. The laws of boat-racing to be observed at the regatta are as follows:—

(The same as the A.R.A. Laws.)

The Amateur Rowing Association

Honourable Secretary: R. C. Lehmann, 30 Bury Street, St James', S.W.

Revised, 23 April 1894.

CONSTITUTION.

I. This Association shall be called 'The Amateur Rowing Association,' and its objects shall be –

1. To maintain the standard of amateur oarsmanship as recognized by the Universities and principal boat clubs of the United Kingdom;
2. To promote the interests of boat-racing generally.

II. The Association shall consist of clubs which adopt the following definition of an amateur, viz.:

No person shall be considered an amateur oarsman, sculler, or coxswain—

1. Who has ever rowed or steered in any race for a stake, money or entrance-fee.

2. Who has ever knowingly rowed or steered with or against a professional for any prize.

3. Who has ever taught, pursued, or assisted in the practice of athletic exercises of any kind for profit.

4. Who has ever been employed in or about boats, or in manual labour, for money or wages.

5. Who is or has been by trade or employment for wages a mechanic, artisan, or labourer, or engaged in any menial duty.

6. Who is disqualified as an amateur in any other branch of sport.

III. Any amateur club willing to bind itself to observe the rules of the Association may become affiliated upon making application to the Hon. Sec. of the A.R.A., and being elected by a majority of two-thirds of the meeting of the Committee.

Every affiliated club shall have at least one vote at General Meetings. Any club having more than two hundred full members shall have in addition one vote for every hundred or part of a hundred members in excess of two hundred; but no club shall have more than six votes.

Every affiliated club shall, when required, send to the Honourable Secretary of the A.R.A. a list of its members and a copy of its last balance sheet.

The Committee shall not consider an application for affiliation from any club previously refused, until after the expiration of twelve calendar months from the date of such refusal.

IV. Each club shall pay to the expenses of the Association an annual subscription to be fixed by the Committee; such subscription not to exceed one guinea.

V. The government and management of the Association shall be vested in a Committee of twenty-five members, who shall meet once at least in every six months, or as often as may be required. At the first meeting of the Committee in each year a chairman shall be elected, who shall remain in office until the next General Meeting. At all meetings of the committee the chairman shall preside, and in his absence a chairman shall be elected for the occasion; seven members shall form a quorum, and the chairman shall have a casting vote.

VI. For the purpose of electing the members of the Committee a General Meeting of the representatives of the affiliated clubs shall be held once a year at a date to be fixed by the Committee. Ten days' notice of this meeting shall be given.

Each club shall notify to the Secretary in writing, not less than three days prior to the Annual General Meeting, the names of its authorized representatives, the number of whom must not exceed the number of votes to which such club is entitled; but should a club nominate one representative only such representative can record the number of votes to which his club is entitled.

VII. Five members of the Committee shall be elected at each Annual General Meeting, and shall remain in office for three years. The Committees of the Cambridge University Boat Club, the Royal Chester Rowing Club, the Kingston Rowing Club, the Leander Club, the London Rowing Club, the Molesey Boat Club, the Oxford University Boat Club, the Thames Rowing Club, and the Twickenham Rowing Cub shall each nominate annually a member of the Committee, and such nomination shall be sent to the Secretary prior to the General Meeting. The Honourable Secretary of the A.R.A. shall be an *ex officio* member of the Committee of the A.R.A. In the year 1894, in order to complete the number of twenty-five, the fifteen members of the Committee elected and nominated as hereinbefore provided shall meet and co-opt the remaining ten members, and the business of that meeting shall be confined to this object alone. Five members of the Committee shall retire annually by rotation, but shall be eligible for re-election. Five of the co-opted members shall retire in 1895, the remaining five in 1896. The Committee shall have power to fill up any vacancy that may occur during the year among the elected members, but any vacancy among the nominated members shall be filled up by the club affected.

VIII. The Committee shall have power to affiliate clubs to the Association, to appoint officers, to make or alter rules, to suspend, disqualify, and reinstate amateurs, and generally to determine and settle all questions and disputes relating to boat racing which may be referred to them for decision. And further, the Committee shall take such other steps as they may consider necessary or expedient for carrying into effect the objects of the Association.

IX. The Committee shall have power on due cause being shown to suspend any affiliated club or to remove it from the list of affiliated clubs.

No motion for the suspension or removal of a club shall be considered except at a Committee Meeting specially called at not less than seven days' notice for the purpose. Such a motion shall not be deemed carried except by a majority of two-thirds of the Committee present.

A resolution for the removal of a club must be confirmed at a subsequent meeting of the Committee specially summoned at not less than seven days' notice for the purpose.

X. The honourable secretary shall be elected by the Committee; he shall keep a proper record of the proceedings of the Committee and of General Meetings, and shall be responsible for the books, accounts, and funds of the Association.

XI. No member of any club affiliated to the Association shall compete in any regatta in England which is not held in accordance with the rules of the Association.

XII. No addition to or alteration in these rules shall be made except by the vote of a majority of two-thirds of a meeting of the Committee specially summoned at not less than seven days' notice for the purpose. Such notice shall state the alteration or addition proposed.

LIST OF AFFILIATED CLUBS

N.B.—The figures denote the number of votes to which each of the clubs is entitled.

(1) Albion Rowing Club.
(1) Anglian Boat Club.
(1) Ariel Rowing Club.
(1) Avon Rowing Club.
(1) Barry Amateur Rowing Club.
(1) Bedford Amateur Rowing Club.
(1) Bewdley Rowing Club.
(1) Birmingham Rowing Club.
(1) Bradford Amateur Rowing Club.
(1) Bridgnorth Rowing Club.
(1) Broxbourne Rowing Club.
(1) Burton Rowing Club.
(6) Cambridge University Boat Club.
(1) Cardiff Amateur Rowing Club.
(1) Cecilian Rowing Club.
(1) Cooper's Hill Boat Club.
(1) Gloucester Rowing Club.
(1) Henley Rowing Club.
(1) Irex Rowing Club.
(1) Iris Rowing Club.
(1) Ironbridge Rowing Club.

(1) Kensington Rowing Club.
(2) Kingston Rowing Club.
(6) Leander Club.
(1) Leicester Rowing Club.
(1) Liverpool Rowing Club.
(6) London Rowing Club.
(1) Marlow Rowing Club.
(1) Medway Rowing Club.
(1) Mersey Rowing Club.
(1) Molesey Boat Club.
(1) North London Boat Club.
(1) Nottingham Rowing Club.
(6) Oxford University Boat Club.
(1) Pembroke Rowing Club.
(2) Pengwern Boat Club.
(1) Reading Rowing Club.
(1) Redcliffe Rowing Club.
(2) Royal Chester Rowing Club.
(1) Royal Savoy Club.
(1) Staines Boat Club.
(1) Stourport Boat Club.
(5) Thames Rowing Club.
(1) Twickenham Rowing Club.
(1) Vesta Rowing Club.
(1) Warwick Boat Club.
(1) Worcester Rowing Club.

RULES FOR REGATTAS.

I. The laws of boat-racing adopted by the Association shall be observed, and the Association's definition of an amateur shall govern the qualifications of each competitor.

II. The Regatta Committee shall state on their programmes, and all other official notices and advertisements, that their regatta is held in accordance with the rules of the A.R.A.

III. No money or 'value prize' (i.e. a cheque on a tradesman) shall be offered for competition, nor shall a prize and money be offered as alternatives.

IV. Entries shall close at least three clear days before the date of the regatta.

V. No assumed name shall be given to the secretary of the regatta unless accompanied by the real name of the competitor.

VI. No one shall enter twice for the same race.

VII. No official of the regatta shall divulge any entry, or report the state of the entrance list, until such list be closed.

VIII. The Regatta Committee shall investigate any questionable entry irrespective of protest, and shall have power to refuse or return any entry up to the time of starting, without being bound to assign a reason.

IX. The captain or secretary of each club or crew entered, shall, at least three clear days before the regatta, deliver to the secretary of the regatta a list containing the names of the actual crew appointed to compete, to which list the names of not more than four other members for an eight-oar, and two for a four-oar, may be added as substitutes.

X. No person may be substituted for another who has already rowed or steered in a heat.

XI. The secretary of the regatta, after receiving the list of the crews entered, and of the substitutes, shall, if required, furnish a copy of the same, with the names, real and assumed, to the captain or secretary of each club or crew entered, and, in the case of pairs or scullers, to each competitor entered.

XII. Objections to the qualification of a competitor must be made in writing to the secretary of the regatta at the earliest moment practicable. No protest shall be entertained unless lodged before the prizes are distributed.

XIII. The whole course must be completed by a competitor before he can be held to have won a trial or final heat.

XIV. In the event of there being but one boat entered for any prize, or if more than one enter and all withdraw but one, the crew of the remaining boat must row over the course to be entitled to such prize.

XV. In the event of a dead heat taking place, any competitor refusing to row again, as may be directed by the Regatta Committee, shall be adjudged to have lost.

XVI. Every competitor must wear complete clothing from the shoulders to the knees – including a sleeved jersey.

XVII. The Regatta Committee shall appoint one or more umpires.

XVIII. The Regatta Committee shall appoint one or more judges, whose decision as to the order in which the boats pass the posts shall be final.

XIX. A maiden oarsman is an oarsman (A) who has never won a race with oars at a regatta; (B) who has never been a competitor in any International or Inter-University Rowing Match.

A maiden sculler is a sculler (A) who has never won a sculling race at a regatta; (B) who has never competed for the Diamond Sculls at Henley, or for the Amateur Championship of any country.

XX. A junior oarsman is an oarsman (A) who has never won a race with oars at a regatta other than a school race; a race in which the construction of the boats was restricted; or a race limited to members of one club; (B) who has never been a competitor in any International or Inter-University match. No oarsman who has won a race at a regatta in which the construction of the boats was restricted, shall compete as a junior in any such race after the end of the current year.

A junior sculler is a sculler (A) who has never won a sculling race at a regatta other than a race in which the construction of the boats was restricted; or a race limited to members of one club; (B) who has never competed for the Diamond Sculls at Henley, or for the Amateur Championship of any country.

N.B. The qualification shall in every case relate to the day of the regatta.

XXI. All questions not specially provided for shall be decided by the Regatta Committee.

LAWS OF BOAT RACING

I. All boat races shall be started in the following manner: – The starter on being satisfied that the competitors are ready, shall give the signal to start.

II. A boat not at its post at the time specified, shall be liable to be disqualified by the umpire.

III. The umpire may act as starter, or not, as he thinks fit; when he does not so act, the starter shall be subject to the control of the umpire.

IV. If the starter considers the start false, he shall at once recall the boats to their stations, and any boat refusing to start again shall be disqualified.

V. Each boat shall keep its own water throughout a race. A boat departing from its own water will do so at its peril.

VI. A boat's own water is its due course, parallel with the course of the other competing boat or boats, from the station assigned to it at starting, to the finish.

VII. No fouling whatever shall be allowed; the boat or boats committing a foul shall be disqualified.

VIII. It shall be considered a foul when, after a race has been started, any competitor, by his oar, boat, or person, comes into contact with the oar, boat, or person of another competitor; unless, in the opinion of the umpire, such contact is so slight as not to influence the race.

IX. A claim of foul must be made to the umpire or the judge by the competitor himself before getting out of his boat.

X. In case of a foul the umpire shall have power

  (a) To place the boats not disqualified in the order in which they come in.

  (b) To order the boats not disqualified to row again on the same or another day.

  (c) To restart the boats not disqualified according to his discretion.

XI. The umpire shall be sole judge of a boat's own water and due course during a race, and he may caution any competitor when in danger of committing a foul.

XII. The umpire, when appealed to, shall decide all questions as to a foul.

XIII. Every boat shall abide by its accidents, but if during a race a boat shall be interfered with by any outside boat, the umpire shall have power, if he thinks fit, to restart the boats according to his discretion, or to order them to row again on the same or another day.

XIV. No boat shall be allowed to accompany or follow any race for the purpose of directing the course of any of the competitors. Any competitor receiving any extraneous assistance may be disqualified, at the discretion of the umpire.

XV. Boats shall be held to have completed the course when their bows reach the winning post.

XVI. Any competitor refusing to abide by the decision of the umpire, or to follow his directions, shall be disqualified.

XVII. The umpire, if he thinks proper, may reserve his decision, provided that in every case such decision be given on the day of the race.

XVIII. The jurisdiction of the umpire extends over a race and all matters connected with it, from the time the race is specified to start until its termination, and his decision in all cases shall be final and without appeal.

A brief explanation of some points arising out of the Rules and Regulations of the A.R.A. may be useful.

Professional

Up to 1894 the A.R.A. gave a very wide interpretation to the term 'professional,' which was held to include 'any person not qualified as an amateur under A.R.A. Rules.' Mechanics, artisans, labourers, men engaged in menial duty, or employed in manual labour for money or wages, were, therefore, not merely disqualified as amateurs, but were considered to be professionals, and competition against them for a prize involved disqualification to the amateur so competing. In 1894, however, the whole code of A.R.A. was submitted to the revision of a sub-committee, and their report, subsequently adopted by the full committee, laid it down that from this time on the word 'professional' must be interpreted 'in its primary and literal sense,' i.e. one who makes money by rowing, sculling, or steering. An amateur rowing, or sculling, or steering with or against a professional for a prize is still disqualified, but the amateur status of one who rows or steers with or against mechanics, artisans, etc. (provided, of course, the race is not for a stake, money, or entrance fee), is not affected. At the same time it must be remembered (Rule I of Rules for Regattas) that at regattas held in accordance with A.R.A. rules no mechanic, artisan, etc., can be admitted to compete, and by Clause XI of the Constitution no member of any club affiliated to the A.R.A. is permitted to compete at a regatta not held in accordance with A.R.A. rules. The result would seem to be, therefore, that whereas an amateur who is not a member of a club affiliated to the A.R.A. can compete against mechanics, artisans, etc., at a regatta not held in accordance with A.R.A. rules without incurring any penalty, a member of a club affiliated to the A.R.A. can compete against this class only in a private match. Any member of an affiliated club transgressing Clause XI would unquestionably render himself liable to suspension under Clause VIII of the Constitution. There are now, therefore, three classes of oarsmen, viz. amateurs, non-amateurs, and professionals.

Non-amateurs

The A.R.A. holds that 'apprenticeship is no disqualification.' Nobody, therefore, is to be disqualified for serving an apprenticeship, even if it involves (as in the case of engineers or nurserymen) manual labour for a money payment. But such manual labour on the part of one who has passed through his ordinary apprenticeship and still continues at the work for a year or two would disqualify.

The committee has held that disqualification attaches, for instance, to –

(1) A watchmaker's assistant who works, or has worked, at the bench.
(2) A baker's assistant who not only helps to make bread, but also delivers it.
(3) Engravers and etchers.
(4) A man having an interest in a boat-letting business, and taking in or starting boats at a raft.

But not to –

(5) A 3rd engineer, sea-going, who goes to sea and works for money, where such sea-service it necessary to qualify him for passing his examinations for the position of chief engineer.
(6) A draughtsman in an engineering firm, though working for wages.

Decisions 3 and 6 are not easily to be reconciled.

Regatta. Junior Oarsmen and Scullers.

Doubts have occasionally arisen as to what is the correct meaning of the word 'Regatta' in Clause XI. of the Constitution, and in Rules 19 and 20 of the Rules for Regattas. The committee has held that any meeting, whether or not called open, at which more than one club, or members of more than one club, compete, is a regatta. This decision does not cover a private match, but does cover a regatta where, for instance, the competition is limited to certain clubs, specially invited by the club or committee who arrange and manage the regatta. Thus, if a junior competed and won, either as an oarsman or sculler, at a regatta limited, say, to members of the London, Kingston, and Thames Rowing Clubs, he would by so winning cease to be a junior, provided the race was neither a school race nor one in which the construction of the boats was restricted.

The committee has decided that a man who rows over for a junior sculls race, even though he receive no prize (the committee not awarding one in any race in which there was only one starter), ceases to be a junior sculler.

A junior sculler may be a senior oarsman, and vice versa.

EXTRACTS FROM THE RULES AND REGULATIONS OF THE CAMBRIDGE UNIVERSITY BOAT CLUB

Laws of the Club

I. That the Cambridge University Boat Club consist of the members of the several boat clubs in the University.

II. That the affairs of the club be under the management of a president, a vice-president (who shall also be hon. secretary), a treasurer, the captains of all boats rowing in the regular university races, and all those who have been members of the University crew. The president and vice-president shall be elected at the first meeting in each term, and those only to be eligible who shall have been members of a university crew. The treasurer shall be a resident graduate of the university, to be elected annually at the first meeting of the Easter Term.

III. That to assist the officers in case of extraordinary and pressing business, a small committee be formed, consisting of the president, vice-president, treasurer, and three extra committee-men, who shall be elected at the last meeting of the C.U.B.C. in each term. That members of the Committee shall have the right of attending meetings of the C.U.B.C. and voting at the same. That at meetings of the committee all except the treasurer must be present in person or by deputy. The treasurer must attend all meetings of the committee on financial questions.

VIII. That all cases of dispute be referred to the president or his deputy, and the four first-boat captains, in residence, of the clubs in their order on the river who are not concerned in the dispute: whose decision shall be final. That representatives of the clubs concerned be present at the meeting.

XVIII. That the secretary of each boat club do send in to the assistant-secretary of the C.U.B.C. a balance-sheet of the receipts and expenditure of his club for the past year, within three weeks of the beginning of the October Term. That the penalty for neglecting this Rule be one guinea.

XIX. That every club do pay to the C.U.B.C. a subscription in proportion to its receipts for the previous year.

XX. That the rate per cent of this tax be fixed by the treasurer of the C.U.B.C., and, when confirmed by the Finance Committee, levied in three equal instalments.

XXI. That all moneys, however obtained, be included in the receipts of a College boat club, except such as are specially subscribed towards the expenses of a crew going to Henley.

XXII. That any club neglecting to pay the subscriptions or arrears due to the C.U.B.C. within six weeks of the beginning of full term be fined one guinea; and that no captain be allowed to vote whose club is in arrears.

XXIII. That medals be given by the C.U.B.C. to each member of such University crews as shall be winners of the University match with Oxford. Also to each member of those College crews which shall be head of the river at the end of the Lent and Easter Term races; and to each member of the Trial Eights.

XXVI. That all boats, except tub-pairs, used for coaching purposes be obliged to carry an India rubber ball fixed to the nose of the boat. That the penalty for neglecting this Rule be one guinea.

Regulations For Boat Racing

I. That none but members of the C.U.B.C. be allowed to row or steer in the C.U.B.C. races.

II. That there be regular eight-oared races in the Easter and Lent Terms, and that the days on which they shall take place and the number of races be appointed and declared at the last general meeting of the preceding term respectively. That in these races two umpires be appointed by the president or his deputy; that in all other C.U.B.C. races one umpire be appointed.

III. That the number of boats be limited in the Easter Term to thirty, rowing in two divisions of fifteen and sixteen respectively, including the sandwich boat, and in the Lent Term to thirty-one, rowing in two divisions of sixteen each, including the sandwich boat.

IV.

(1) That in the Lent and Easter Terms the two divisions be named respectively first and second division. That in the Lent Term both divisions shall row in clinker-built boats not more than 57 feet long, with not less than five streaks on a side, none of which shall exceed 4½ inches (outside measurement). All such boats must be passed by the president and secretary of the C.U.B.C. before they can be used in the races. That in the Easter Term the first division shall row in racing ships on sliding seats, and the second division in clinker-built boats, as above, and sliding seats.

(2) That every college boat club have the right to be represented by at least one boat in the Lent races; and by at least one, and not more than three, in the May races.

V. That during the races no person shall row or steer in both divisions (the crews of the last boats in a division excepted), except under peculiar circumstances, to be decided by the president or his deputy and the four senior captains in residence who are not concerned, which decision must be obtained before the crew or crews in question be allowed to start.

VI. In the races in the Lent Term no one be allowed to row or steer who rowed or steered respectively in any race of the previous Easter Term.

VII. That no one be allowed to row in the Lent or May races, or Fours or Pairs, after more than four years have elapsed from the first term he came up, unless he keep in residence three-fourths of the term in which he desires to row.

VIII. That each crew be chosen from one club and college in the case of Trinity and St John's, and from not more than two clubs or two colleges in the case of other colleges; and that the crew of the two colleges joining be considered as a fresh one, and start from the bottom.

IX. That in order to take a boat off the river the captain must give notice to the honourable secretary of the C.U.B.C., who shall place lists of the boats entered for the races, arranged according to their order, in the different university boathouses, at least a week before the commencement of races in each term, and on every race day during the term.

X.

(1) That in the Easter Term any club desirous of putting on a second or third boat shall have the right to challenge the lowest non-representative boat to a bumping race, but if successful shall start at the bottom of the river. That if there be more challenging crews than one, they shall row a time race among themselves, and the winner shall row the challenged boat. That the entrance fee for such races be five guineas; that the date for them be fixed at the first general meeting of the term, and that at least ten clear days' notice be given to the secretary of the C.U.B.C. by the captains of crews desirous to compete.

(2) That no man who has rowed in the successful challenging boat shall row in a higher boat during the following May races, except as in Chapter III, rule 7.

XI. That the boats row down to their stations in reversed order, the last boat of each division starting first.

XII. That on racing days in the Lent Term a gun be fired at the Railway Bridge, at 3.00 p.m., as a signal for the last boat of the second division to row down; at 3.15 p.m. for the first boat of the division; and a third at 4.00 p.m. for the first boat of the first division. That in the Easter Term corresponding signals be fired for the second and first division boats at 5.00 p.m., 5.15 p.m., and 6.15 p.m. respectively. That boats starting late be fined one guinea.

That at the close of each race of the second division in the Lent Term, and of the second division in the Easter Term, a gun be fired at the Bridge; and that until this gun be fired no boat of the other racing division shall pass below the Ash Plantation under penalty of one guinea. That the umpire be responsible for the punctual firing of these guns. That any racing boat, leaving so late as to be obliged to pass the first boat of its division below Ditton Corner, be fined one guinea by the captain of the latter on behalf of the C.U.B.C. That the captain of the first boat starting late, or neglecting to act as this rule directs, be fined one guinea.

XIII. That the races be bumping races, and the starting posts be 175 feet apart. That the last post be at Baitsbite-lock, and the winning posts at the Big Horse-grind and the first ditch above the Railway Bridge.

XIV. That the first seven boats in all divisions be obliged to go up to the further post at the Big Horse-grind, and the other boats be obliged to stop at the nearer post at the first ditch above the Railway Bridge; also that the eighth boats have the option of stopping at the nearer or going on to the further post.

XV. That each boat start with the coxswain holding a line 36 feet in length attached to its post (or, if he by chance lose the line, with No. 7's rowlock opposite the post); that otherwise it cannot make a bump, but is subject to be bumped and to be fined one guinea.

XVI. That if a boat miss a race, the boat behind it shall row past its post and be allowed the bump, and that the boat missing the race be fined one guinea.

XVII. That the boats be started by three guns: the first gun shall be fired when the head boat shall have arrived at its post, the order being given by the captain of that boat; the second gun three minutes after the first, and the last gun one minute after the second.

XVIII. That a boat be considered fairly bumped when it is touched by any part of the boat behind it, before its stern is past the winning-post; passing a boat being equivalent to a bump, providing the passing boat draw its whole length in advance. (The word boat includes the ship, crew, and oars, if in rowlock.) That the coxswain of a boat so bumped shall immediately acknowledge the bump by holding up his hand, and that the crew making the bump immediately cease rowing; that any crew neglecting this rule be fined one guinea.

XIX. That when one boat bumps another, both shall immediately draw aside till the racing boats have passed; that the last boat carry a white flag in the bows; that any boat neglecting this rule be fined one guinea.

XX. That if one boat bumps another they exchange places, whatever may have been their position before starting. That any boat making a bump may row up after the race with its flag hoisted; as also the boat rowing head.

XXI. That in order to claim a bump, the captain, on arriving at the Goldie Boathouse, must bracket the bump, state where it took place, and sign his name on the secretary's list; if the bump be not bracketed he shall be fined one guinea, but that the bumps shall, on sufficient evidence, be allowed; and that no bumps can be claimed after six o'clock in the Lent Term, or after nine in the Easter Term, or disputed after nine on the following morning.

XXII. That all cases of disputed bumps be referred to the president, or his deputy, and the four first-boat captains, in residence, of the clubs in their order on the river who are not concerned in the dispute, whose decision shall be final; and who shall have the power, in all doubtful cases, of causing the boats concerned to row the race again, starting from their original posts; and that there be representatives at the meeting of the clubs interested in the dispute.

XXV. That watermen be allowed to coach members of College boats in tub-pairs only till within a fortnight of the first day of the races.

XXVII. That breaches of Regulations issued by the officers of the C.U.B.C. be liable to a fine of one guinea.

Lent Term Races and Time Races

I. That all clubs wishing to put another boat on the river must enter such boat with the secretary of the C.U.B.C. on or before a date to be appointed by him at the beginning of the Lent Term.

Entrance fee, three guineas, to be paid at the time of entry.

II. That the Rules for these races be the same as those for the 'Getting-on' races in the Easter Term, and that the races be under the management of the C.U.B.C. or their deputies [see chapter II, rule 10 (1)].

III. That no first boat of a club be obliged to row for its place.

IV. That these races be rowed on days preceding the Lent races.

V. That no man shall row in these time races (1) who has rowed on any night of the previous May races, or (2) who does not comply with Chapter II, rule 7.

VI. That no man who has rowed in the successful boat or boats during these trial time-races shall row in a higher boat in the following Lent races, except under peculiar circumstances, to be decided upon by the president, or his deputy, and the four senior captains in residence who are not concerned.

VII. That when more than two boats start in a heat to race for getting on the river, such heat be started by three guns: the first gun to be fired when the last boat to come down shall have arrived at its post, the order being given by the umpire; the second gun three minutes after the first, and the last one minute after the second. That chains 36 feet in length be provided 100 yards apart. That each boat start with the coxswain holding the chain allotted to it (or, if he by chance lose the chain, with No. 7's rowlock opposite the post), that otherwise it is liable to be disqualified.

VIII. That in time races, under the management of the C.U.B.C., the pistols at the winning posts be fired by university men, who shall be called on to do so in the following order:—

The president, secretary, and committee of the C.U.B.C.; then the first captain of the boats in their order on the river, or deputies from their own clubs; provided that no one of the same club as any of the competitors shall fire a pistol in any race in which such competitor of his own club is rowing; and that no one need, by reason of this rule, refuse to umpire. And that to prevent all difficulties of a pistol missing fire, a second person be appointed by the President or his deputy to stand at each winning post and hold up a white flag, which shall be dropped the moment that the nose of the boat passes the post.

IX. That in time races no boat draw more than one bye.

X. That if in any time race any boat touch any part of, or pass on the course, or be in any way inconvenienced by any boat in front of it, and the boat so touching, passing, or being inconvenienced, shall not come to its post first in order, such boat shall be allowed to start in the following day's race, whether the same would otherwise have been a final or a trial heat, and shall start on the same footing as regards drawing for stations, etc., as the other boats left in.

Or the boat so impeded shall row again with the boat coming in first.

Rules for the University Clinker Fours

I. That the University Clinker-built Fours be rowed as time races over the Colquhoun course.

II. That the race be open to crews from any club, such crews to be composed solely of men who did not row in the first division of the previous May races.

III. That no 'Blue' be allowed to compete.

IV. That the coxswains must be members of the clubs they steer, and must weigh not less than 7 stone 7 lbs.

V. The definition of a clinker boat is as follows:– That no boat have less than five streaks on a side, none of which shall exceed 4½ inches (outside measurement). All such boats must be passed by the president and secretary of the C.U.B.C. at least one week before the commencement of the races.

VI. That the entrance money for each boat be one guinea.

Laws of the Magdalene Silver Pair-Oars and University

Presentation Cups

I. That watermen be allowed to coach and steer for these races.

IV. That any member qualified to pull in the C.U.B.C. races be qualified to start for these oars.

V. That the crews need not consist of members of one club.

VI. That no winning pair be allowed to enter together a second time.

Regulations of the 'Colquhoun Silver Sculls'

III. That only those members of the C.U.B.C. who have not exceeded five years from the date of their first commencing residence be allowed to start, on complying with the terms herein specified.

EXTRACTS FROM THE RULES AND REGULATIONS OF THE OXFORD UNIVERSITY BOAT CLUB

General Rules

I. That the club be open to all members of the university on the following conditions: –

II. That any graduate of the university by paying two pounds, or any undergraduate by paying £3 10s, may become a life member.

III. That any member of the university by paying one pound may become a member for one term, not being thereby qualified to row or steer in any of the university races unless he has paid four such terminal subscriptions.

IV. That the subscription must be paid before the admission to the club.

V. That this club is affiliated to the Amateur Rowing Association, and that members are therefore bound to observe the A.R.A. rules.

VII. That the officers of the club consist of president, secretary, and treasurer; who, with two other members of the club, shall form a committee.

VIII. That no member who is not strictly residing be on the committee.

IX. That the president, secretary, treasurer, and committee be elected by the captains of College boat clubs, or their representatives.

X. That the election of the president and secretary take place at the first captains' meeting in the Summer Term, that of the treasurer and the other members of the committee at the first meeting in the October Term.

XI. That the president have the entire supervision of the property of the club; that he preside over all captains' meetings; have the sole selection and management of all university crews, and that he have absolute authority and entire responsibility in all matters immediately concerning the University boat; that he have charge of the president's book, and make such records in it as shall be interesting and useful to the future of the club; and that he keep the official records of all University races.

XXV. That if Henley Regatta do not take place at such a date in relation to Commemoration Day as is convenient to the O.U.B.C., the club reserves to itself the right of withdrawing its subscription.

XXVI. That the racing boat last purchased be not let or sold under any circumstances whatever.

Rules for Races
I. That all future members of the O.U.B.C. shall show a certificate of having passed a satisfactory swimming test before being allowed to row in university races.

II. That such certificate be either (1) that of some public school approved by the committee, or (2) a certificate from Dolley's Baths, signed by the bathman, and countersigned by the captain of the College boat club.

III. That any College boat club rowing a member who has obtained a certificate unfairly shall be fined five pounds, and lose one place on the river for each night on which he has rowed.

IV. That each college shall have its own punt and waterman during the races.

V. That the captain of each boat club shall, so far as possible, fix upon the maximum number which his punt is able to carry, and that this number shall in no case exceed twelve, and that the fine for overcrowding be 5s.

VI. That each barge shall be furnished with two lifebuoys.

VII. That the bows of all racing Eights and Fours, both keelless and clinker-built, and of all racing pair-oars and sculling boats be protected by an India rubber ball, and the penalty for violation of this rule be, in the case of Eights and Fours, one pound; in the case of all other boats, 10s.

VIII. That all Challenge Cups which are the property of the O.U.B.C. shall either be taken home by the captain of the boat club which holds them, or be deposited at Rowell and Harris's during the vacation.

The Eights and Torpids

I. That all gentlemen rowing or steering in the races must be life members of the O.U.B.C.

II. That no boat be allowed to start in the races with more or less than eight oars.

III. That all boats starting in the races carry a coxswain over the whole course.

IV. That the names of the crews be sent to the treasurer at least one day before the races begin, and that afterwards no change can be made, unless notice is given to the president at least one hour before the races begin, under a penalty of one pound.

V. That every club neglecting to send in the names of its crew to the treasurer, and pay the entrance money, five pounds, into the Old Bank, on or before the day previous to the first race in which they intend to row, shall forfeit five shillings; and that every club entering a boat after the races have begun shall pay one pound for every night of the races on which it has not had a boat on.

VI. That no club start a boat in the races till all its arrears are paid, whether of fines, entrance money, or annual subscription.

VII. That no crew be allowed to start in the races which shall have employed any waterman in capacity of coach or trainer within three weeks of the first race.

VIII. That no college be allowed to enter more than one boat for the Eights, unless it has had on a Torpid in the same year.

IX. That each boat start from a rope held by the steerer, and fastened to a post on the Berkshire shore; the rope to be 50 feet in length.

X. That the last boat be stationed above Iffley Lasher; and that 130 feet be the distance between the posts.

XI. That the boats entered for the races be divided as equally as possible, and row in two divisions; that the second division row first, and never contain fewer boats than the first division; that the head boat of the second division may row again with first division; and that the last boat of the first division start head of the second division on the following day.

XII. That the president provide a starter, who shall fire a signal gun for the boats to take their places; after four minutes another gun; and after the interval of one minute another gun for the start; after the third gun the race be always held to have begun.

XIII. That any boat starting before the gun goes off do lose a place forthwith.

XIV. That when a boat touches the boat or any part of the boat before it, or its oars or rudder, it be considered a bump; and also if a boat rows clean by another it be equivalent to a bump.

XV. That both the boat which bumps and the boat which is bumped immediately row out of the course of the other racing boats; and in case any obstruction be caused by culpable neglect of this, the offending boat be fined five pounds.

XVI. That after every bump the boat bumping change places with the boat bumped, whatever be their orders before starting; also in a bumping race no boat can make more than one bump, but of four boats, A, B, C, D, should B bump C, then A may bump D, and the next race A and D change places with each other.

XVII. That in the case of any boat not starting, the boat immediately behind them do row past their starting-post and be considered to have bumped the other boat.

XVIII. That all boats stand by their accidents; and that, in case of dispute, boats must take the place assigned them by the committee.

XIX. That an umpire be appointed by the first six colleges of each division in rotation, who shall sit and vote on the committee to decide disputes on the day on which he is in authority.

XX. That the races finish at the lower of the white posts to which Salter's barge is moored, on which a flag is to be hoisted, and that a boat is liable to be bumped till every part of it has passed that post, and that a judge be appointed by the president.

XXI. That if any boat after passing the post impedes another which has not passed the post, it be fined £5.

XXVI. That all disputes concerning bumps, etc., arising out of the races, be referred to the committee on the day of the race, who shall decide the point before the next race.

XXVIII. That the College races take place in Easter or Act Term, and be six in number.

XXIX. That no non-resident member of the University may either row or steer in the races, unless he has resided in Oxford at least ten consecutive days before the races commence. That this rule apply to all University races, viz. Eights, Torpids, Fours, Pairs, and Sculls.

XXX. That no one may be allowed to row or steer in the races for a college or hall of which he is not a bona fide member.

XXXI.—That a man may be held to have rowed or steered in the Eights or Torpids when he has so officiated for three days.

Torpid Races – Special Rules

That the Torpid races be regulated by the above rules as far as they are applicable: but

(1) That the races take place in the Lent Term, and be six in number.

(2) That no one who has rowed or steered in the Eights may officiate in the same capacity in the next Torpid races.

(3) That no one be allowed to row in his Torpid who has exceeded sixteen terms from his Matriculation.

(4) That unless a college has had an Eight on the river more than three nights during the previous year, it be not permitted to start a Torpid, unless it engage to put on a distinct Eight in the ensuing Eights.

That in this case the distinct Eight

(a) Do contain five men, at least, who have not rowed in the Torpids.

(b) Be compelled to row more than three nights, under penalty of £10.

(5) That the committee have power to relax this rule at their discretion in the case of boats in the second division.

(6) That these races be rowed in gig boats, of the specified mould, measuring inside at the gunwale not less than 2 feet 2 inches, clinker-built of not less than 5 streaks.

(7) That the distance between the starting posts be 160 feet.

(8) That no Torpid be allowed to use sliding seats.

(9) That if more than twenty-five Torpids enter, the races shall be in three divisions; the boats to be divided as equally as possible, so that a higher division shall not contain more boats than a lower one.

Four-Oar Challenge Cup

I. That the Cup be open for competition to members of any one college or hall who have not exceeded eighteen terms from their Matriculation.

II. That the race take place annually, in the Michaelmas Term.

VII. That no crew be allowed to start which has had any waterman in the capacity of "coach" or trainer within three weeks of the first race.

Clinker Fours Race

I. That the race be called the 'Clinker Fours' race.

II. That the race take place annually in the Lent Term.

III. That it should be open for competition to members of any college or hall who have not exceeded eighteen terms from their Matriculation, and who have not rowed either in the University Race at Putney, or the Trials, or rowed in a College Eight which finished in the upper division of the summer races in the previous year, sandwich boat reckoning as Second Division.

IV. That the race shall be rowed in keeled clinker-built boats with slides of not more than 12 inches, having not less than 5 streaks in each side, exclusive of saxe-board. The streaks shall not be more than 4¼ inches in breadth. The maximum inside width of each boat shall not be less than 24 inches, measured on the top of the gunwale. No batswings, false outriggers, splayed-boards, or other device will be allowed to take the place of saxe-boards, and the committee of the O.U.B.C. reserve the right of determining in each instance whether these conditions have been fairly carried out or not.

V. That no boat be allowed to start with more or less than four oars and a coxswain.

VI. That no crew be allowed to start which has had any waterman in the capacity of 'coach' or trainer.

RULES FOR THE UNIVERSITY TRIAL EIGHT RACE

I. That the race be called the 'University Trial Eight Race.'

II. That the race take place in Michaelmas Term, and subsequent to that for the Four-Oared Challenge Cup.

III. That the crews be selected by the president.

IV. That the crews be in practice not less than twelve days.

V. That each member of the two crews pay 10s entrance money.

VI. That a silver medal be presented to each of the winning crew.

VII. That any member of the two crews who refuses to row in the University Eight if called upon to do so, be suspended by the committee from rowing in any University race till the end of the Summer Term, unless he shows reasonable grounds for refusal.

Some Sports Stand the Test of Time

Classic Guides

from Amberley Publishing

The
Classic Guide
to
CRICKET

W. G. GRACE

The
Classic Guide
to
FOOTBALL

C. W. ALCOCK

The
Classic Guide
to
TENNIS

JOHN MOYER HEATHCOTE

The
Classic Guide
to
GOLF

HORACE GORDON HUTCHINSON

The
Classic Guide
to
SAILING

E. F. KNIGHT

Find us on Facebook
facebook.com/amberleybooks

Follow us on Twitter
@amberleybooks

w. www.amberley-books.com   **T.** +44 1453 847800   **E.** sales@amberley-books.com